P9-DVH-766

A PICTORIAL HISTORY OF

Jazz

A PICTORIAL HISTORY OF
JAZZ

PEOPLE AND PLACES
FROM NEW ORLEANS TO THE SIXTIES

Compiled by
ORRIN KEEPNEWS
and
BILL GRAUER, JR.

Text and Captions by
ORRIN KEEPNEWS

Second Edition Revised by
ORRIN KEEPNEWS

With a New Foreword

BONANZA BOOKS • NEW YORK

ACKNOWLEDGMENTS: for the 1966 edition

In revising this book, the major emphasis has been on the events and people of the past decade, and on the decade before that as now seen in clearer perspective. Thus the principal need for assistance was from those who have been active on the recent and current scene. All pleas for help were answered by such people with speed and an almost overwhelming degree of cooperation. But for extraordinary assistance in several ways, very special thanks must go to the following:

To Steve Schapiro for so many of his fine photographs, for rare patience, and for instruction in how to look at negatives; to Chuck Stewart for *his* fine photographs and his thoughtfulness; to Jack Bradley for making available both his own camera work and his impressive collection. Also to Robert Asen, who was publisher of the late *Metronome* magazine, for throwing open those files; to Pete Welding and Don DeMichael of *Down Beat* for tricky cooperation via the mails, and additional thanks to Welding for further photographs of his own making and from his personal collection; to Dom Cerulli and Art Hawck of the advertising agency for MGM and Verve Records for so politely permitting the looting of their picture files; and to Bob Altshuler and Frank Driggs of Columbia Records, and Nesuhi Ertegun of Atlantic for much the same thing. Don Schlitten was most helpful, and Dan Morgenstern made some very valuable recommendations.

To thank Leonard Feather and George Hoefer for being cooperative is almost redundant—any other behavior from either is impossible to imagine. Finally, to Lucy and Peter and David Keepnews, for answering silly questions during the selecting of photos but never asking any.

Although the late Bill Grauer was not involved in these revisions, it should be clear that his tremendous contributions to the original conception and creation of this book remain undiminished. A considerable debt of gratitude should also be noted to the late Bob Simon, a fine editor and publisher, who helped bring the book into existence in the first place.

O.K.

New York City
February, 1966

ACKNOWLEDGMENTS: for the first edition

It should be obvious that the compilation of a volume such as this would have been impossible without the cooperation of a great many people. Although we were able to draw freely from the extensive picture files of *The Record Changer* magazine, we were also dependent to a large extent on the helpfulness and generosity of musicians, collectors and authorities in various fields of jazz. Everyone to whom we turned proved eager (rather than merely willing) to be of assistance, and we are pleased to make note here of our extreme indebtedness to all of them.

George Hoefer, who has for many years conducted the "Hot Box" column in *Down Beat*, graciously placed at our disposal his very large collection of rare photographs. Dr. Edmond Souchon; David Stuart; Turk Murphy; Tony Parenti; Duncan Scheidt; Nat Shapiro; Frederic Ramsey, Jr.; Leonard Feather; and in particular Jack Tracy, editor of *Down Beat*, and Bill Coss, editor of *Metronome*, all provided more than a few pictures of considerable value that would otherwise have been unobtainable.

We are most grateful also, for photographs and/or other important assistance, to Louis Armstrong, Moe Asch, George Avakian, Paul Bacon, Mr. and Mrs. Count Basie, Charles Campbell, Roy J. Carew, Helen Chmura, Thomas A. Dorsey, Al Eiseman, Hank Eisner, Nesuhi Ertegun, Hal Flakser, Anne Fulchino and the publicity department of RCA-Victor, Bob Greene, Peggy Hale, John Hammond, Jim Heanue, Lester Koenig, Bob Koester, Bob Lee, Lom LeGoullon, J. Robert Mantler, Thelonious Monk, Walter Page, Bob Parent, the Herman Rosenberg Collection and Stanley Rosenberg, Bill Russell, Cecil Scott, Millicent Scott, Mr. and Mrs. Joe Sullivan, Charles Sutherland, Billy Taylor, Mr. and Mrs. George Wallington, Randy Weston, and George Wettling. Our wives, Lucile Keepnews and Jane Grauer, can never be thanked sufficiently for suggestions, criticisms, and moral support, and for learning to put up with the odd hours we have been using as our normal working day.

O.K.
B.G., Jr.

New York City
October, 1955

This edition is published by Bonanza Books, distributed by Crown Publishers, Inc.

h g f e d c b a

1981 EDITION

Manufactured in the United States of America

Library of Congress Cataloging in Publication Data

Keepnews, Orrin.
  A pictorial history of jazz.

  Reprint.
  1. Jazz music—Pictorial works. 2. Jazz
musicians—Portraits. I. Grauer, Bill, 1922-
1963. II. Title.
ML3506.K44   1981 785.42′0973 81-10242
ISBN 0-517-000091   AACR2

Table of Contents

FOREWORD TO THE 1981 REPRINT

A Pictorial History of Jazz is now more than a quarter of a century old. In 1955, when it was originally brought into being by the late Bill Grauer and myself, I was very much a beginner in the jazz world. While I had spent many years as a fan and several as a writer, I had barely begun to be occupied with what turned out to be my true jazz calling and still ongoing career as a record producer. Eleven years later, when I was asked to prepare a revised edition, I had become thoroughly immersed in that profession. This meant, among other things, that many of my attitudes and opinions had altered and that I was much more deeply aware of how quickly the "present" becomes the "past" in this constantly changing music. This led me to do some touching up of early sections of the book, to recast the last several chapters, and in particular to completely reshape and greatly expand the last two. I was proud of the book when it first appeared; after completing the revisions, I remained quite pleased with both the new and the unchanged portions.

Now, quite suddenly, a lot more time has passed and it is 1981. My recording activities, I should note, have always involved a certain amount of reissuing of older jazz classics. In recent years, somewhat to my surprise, the term *older jazz classics* has gradually expanded to include records originally produced by me. Where once the source material for reissues had only been the discs of such as Jelly Roll Morton and Louis Armstrong and Bix Beiderbecke, by now Thelonious Monk and Wes Montgomery, Cannonball Adderley and Bill Evans (to limit the examples only to artists I have worked with) have become fit subjects for rerelease. In addition to making me feel just a touch schizophrenic, this has led me to some very strongly felt conclusions about reissues. One of the strongest has to do with the tremendous importance of preserving a sense of the original time and context: do not put a current photo on an album of a musician's work of twenty years ago; do not obscure by so-called enhancement the intrinsic truth of the recorded sound of a somewhat earlier day.

Now, logically enough, this same concept of reissue is being applied here. To bring this history "up to date" would not only be a foredoomed effort (I learned long ago that today's jazz update must by tomorrow again revert to being out-of-date), but it would represent a rather pointless wrenching of most of the chapters out of the time frame in which they were constructed.

I can assure you (if such assurance is really needed) that I know all too well how many people referred to in the present tense in these pages are no longer living: Louis and Duke, and quite a few much younger men, including some who were among my dearest friends and closest associates. I know also that there are those who receive only passing mention here but have in the intervening years become major contributors to the growth and life of the music. There are those not named or pictured at all, either because of my 1966 lack of foresight or because they were not yet even on the scene; and still others who—from the temporary vantage point of this moment in time—appear to have been overvalued back then. But all this is precisely what is meant by preserving the original context. I am still as proud of the book in an overall sense as I was in 1966 (even though I surely know its shortcomings better than anyone else), and much more pleased with this verbatim reprinting than I could be with any patchwork attempt to make it "current."

As a faithful reproduction of a work that has been out of print long enough to become a collector's item, its only negative aspect is for secondhand dealers who probably can no longer ask mind-boggling prices for a rare old original copy. That has a comforting air of consistency about it: I can readily recall the anger of certain rare-record collectors back in 1953 when Grauer and I began reissuing Ma Rainey and King Oliver and such on 10-inch Riverside albums, thereby greatly devaluing their original 78-rpm records— but at the same time making the music much more widely accessible.

Among the obligations of a reissue is to remind you that all the gratitude previously expressed is still specifically in effect. The acknowledgments to the first and the revised editions, now reprinted on page iv, are as heartfelt as ever, as is my appreciation of the courtesies extended by all the picture sources (page 297). In addition, new thanks to Alan Mirken of Crown Publishers/Bonanza Books for stubbornly insisting that it was more than time for this book to be generally available again.

ORRIN KEEPNEWS

San Francisco
May, 1981

INTRODUCTION

This book follows, for the most part, a historical sequence: "people and places from New Orleans to modern jazz." However, there is a certain amount of overlapping of time and place within and between our various subdivisions; also, where it seemed best to devote a chapter to a single individual or to a form of jazz not particularly limited to any precise period (Louis Armstrong, for example, or the blues), we have departed from strict chronology and used logic rather than consistency of format as our guide. It should also be noted that we have chosen, as chapter headings, song titles that seem relevant to the subject matter and descriptive of it.

We have delved into our own accumulations of photographs and assorted oddments; we have induced some friends and some musicians to do likewise; we have researched in various places; and we have turned to several people and organizations, as noted in the acknowledgments. Still, we make no claim to a "complete" history. There are inevitable gaps; the photographs that should have been taken but never were; much worse, those that should have been preserved but apparently were not; probably worst of all, the wonderful pictures that will not turn up until this book is already in print, and the pictures that lie in places where we should have thought to look, but didn't. Allow us to note, then, that the first word of our title is not "The," but "A." There are also limitations that are self-imposed, by choice: being basically a collection of pictures, this volume does not attempt to describe in as much detail, state as dogmatically, or analyze as deeply as a work made up entirely of words might do. There are further limitations we cannot hope to see: those attributable to our personal tastes, emphases and bias (although we like to think of ourselves as being most eclectic and unbiased). None of the foregoing, however, is in any sense an apology. This book has come into being because we are and have for a long time been fascinated by jazz—in virtually all of its many manifestations. This particular contribution of ours to jazz lore is a product of our experience and our affection, and we are more than a little proud of it.

The book can perhaps best be described as a sort of family album of jazz—an attempt to gather together a substantial number of graphic mementos of this unique American music. Jazz is, of course, essentially self-descriptive; it is music, and the first and truest way to know it is to hear it. But that is not the only way.

Jazz has always served as an expression of people and of their environment—of a great many different people who have created it and reacted to it, in a great many different settings. Perhaps the truest measure of the validity of jazz is that it can be all things to all men: a mild form of amusement; an emotional or an intellec-

tual stimulant; an art form; a social commentary; a cult; something to like, love, or even hate for a wide variety of esthetic, emotional or social reasons. Thus jazz is both simple (no more than the combinations of notes you hear) and incredibly complex (as complex as human beings and as the world we inhabit). And thus it is a fit subject for all the analysis, history, biography, criticism and what-have-you that has been built up alongside it.

It is somewhat startling to note that this is still a very young music. The span between the first and last chapters of this book is, roughly, seven decades; precisely how short a time this is can be made quite clear by pointing out that at least a few men who were on hand to hear and to take part in its earliest stages are still more or less active performers as this is written (Louis Armstrong, Kid Ory, George Brunies are names that come to mind). On the other hand, this span of time, though no more than a man's full lifetime, has also been a period of vast and sweeping changes in American life. Probably the truly startling point is not that jazz has altered so much in so short a time, but rather that a music so intensely personal and so strongly affected by its environment has not changed to an even greater extent. For there are still quite recognizable bonds and links that make it possible accurately to call all of it—from Buddy Bolden to Benny Goodman to Charlie Parker and beyond—part of the same music.

Jazz, then, is many things (simple, complex; young, old; changing, constant). Much fact and argument have been written down about it; and a vast amount of all its forms is readily available to the ear, either "live" or on records. Considering all this, it seems high time for a survey directed at the eye. Individual men and women played and are playing this music; they inhabited specific cities at specific times; they worked in this dingy bar and that barn of a dance hall. At the very least, the value of a pictorial review is that it can help make these people stay alive or come alive again for the audience that listens to jazz and reads about it—it can help keep the people of jazz from becoming merely disembodied sounds or names.

But like jazz itself, a book such as this one can be taken in any number of ways: as historical documentation, as an illustration of the rise (or decline) of an art form; as the record of one aspect of the changing cultural or social scene in this country; as a picture gallery of great men and lesser men and figures of legend; or as an album to be leafed through for the pleasure of colorful snatches of glamour or excitement, of nostalgia or remembrance or discovery. Our personal preference is for the last interpretation, but that of course is nothing that need bind you. Here are the faces and the scenes of jazz; make of them what you will. . . .

NEVER CLOSED

TOM ANDERSON'S
Annex

COR. BASIN & IBERVILLE STS.

NOTED THE STATES
OVER *for* BEING THE
BEST CONDUCTED
CAFE *in* AMERICA

PRIVATE ROOMS *for the* FAIR SEX

MUSIC NIGHTLY

PHONES: 2253-Y & 2993-W

BILLY STRUVE, *Manager*

New Orleans Joys

STORYVILLE WAS its spawning ground, the streets of New Orleans its first home. There can be no precise date for the birth of jazz, for it came into being by a slow process of accumulation—the gradual fusion of many different strains and the impact of many different personalities. But by the turn of the century, and largely in the city of New Orleans, the music now called jazz (but which was not then known by that name, or by any single name) was taking recognizable shape.

In the background lay the tribal rhythms of African ancestors; the work songs of Southern field hands; the spirituals and gospel music that were the Negro's own interpretation of the white man's religion; the rich and plaintive sound of the blues; the stomps, probably derived from folk dances; the pulsing syncopation of ragtime. There were the brass bands, white and Negro, that marched in parades and gave picnic-grounds concerts, and there was the Creoles' music, rich with French and Spanish influences. All this and more played a part in the development of this melting-pot of a music.

The sprawling, bustling port at the mouth of the Mississippi was the Big City, drawing the restless, the greedy and the talented from a wide surrounding area. New Orleans was also a city with a heavy share of what is known as "vice." In 1897, this activity was confined by law to a mere thirty-eight blocks in the French Quarter, in which prostitution, though not exactly legal, was openly tolerated. This was Storyville, known also as The District. Here flourished the brothels—and the gambling joints, saloons, dives and cabarets that clustered around them. It was here that the newly emerging music flourished, too, furnishing a keynote for all this high and low life.

It is easy to overdo the jazz-and-vice connection, however. Much more than just a honky-tonk music, jazz was an integral part of New Orleans Negro life. It meant street parades, with the brass bands strutting in the hot sunlight ("King" Joe Oliver blasting away, with a handkerchief under the uniform hat to absorb the sweat). It meant bands riding through town on trucks to advertise a dance (with the tailgate down and young Kid Ory's big trombone reaching out over it). It meant the funeral processions, among the most colorful of New Orleans memories (the band playing dirges out to the cemetery, then stomping a tune like *Didn't He Ramble* on the way back). In a large sense, though, it was all one music. For the men who paraded by day were, for the most part, those who worked in the joints of The District at night.

Some of these musicians are now little more than legend-shrouded names: like Buddy Bolden, the barber who was the first great cornetist and who died in an insane asylum. Others, only slightly younger, are still very much with us: like Louis Armstrong, most famous of the boys who grew up with the sound of jazz all around them. Theirs was a rough life rather than a glamorous one, even though legend has put a nostalgic veil around the bare dance halls where Bolden pounded out his low-down blues, and around dives like the 601 Ranch (which, after the owner was killed in a brawl, soon reopened as the 602 Ranch). And the men who earned their living in such places were obviously unaware that they were carving out the foundations of what can surely be called America's most valid musical form—but as it turned out, that was exactly what they were doing.

A 1906 advertisement for a noted Storyville Cafe.

The cruel fact is that if there had been no Negro slavery, there would have been no jazz. Africans came to this country crowded onto the decks of slave ships *(top)*; families were torn apart when some members were "Sold to Go South," which is the title of the mid-page scene. The bottom photo shows a portion of 19th-century New Orleans.

NEW ORLEANS LA.

New Orleans in the days when jazz was being born. The top picture shows Canal Street, the main thoroughfare, in the very early 1900s, with the celebrated French Opera House on the far side of the street. At the bottom: the outlying resort area of Milneburg, where many bands played.

The only known picture of the legendary Buddy Bolden *(standing, second from left)*, taken sometime before 1895. His can certainly be considered the first of all jazz bands. Other members included valve trombonist Willie Cornish, shown at Bolden's left, and clarinetist Frank Lewis *(seated)*.

When Bolden's mind snapped in about 1907 (some said from overwork, some said women), his band was taken over by trombonist Frankie Duson (also spelled Dusen). This rare snapshot of Frank, which also seems to have served him as an advertising card, was taken a bit later, probably in 1923.

6

Willie "Bunk" Johnson was one of most respected of early cornetists. Here he is *(standing, second from left)* in the Original Superior Orchestra. For Bunk at a much later age, see Chapter 17.

All the early bands had fine, proud names. This is the Imperial Band, with "Big Eye" Louis Nelson *(center)* on clarinet, and cornetist Manuel Perez *(rear, right)*.

PREFACE
"A Word to The Wise"

The author of this Directory and Guide of the Tenderloin District has been before the people on many occasions as to his authority on what is doing in the "Queer Zone"—Tenderloin.

Everyone who knows to-day from yesterday will say that my Blue Book is the goods right from the spring.

WHY NEW ORLEANS SHOULD HAVE THIS DIRECTORY.

First. Because it is the only district of its kind in the States set aside for the fast women by *law*.

Second. Because it puts the stranger on a proper grade or path as to where to go and be secure from hold-ups, brace games and other illegal practices usually worked on the unwise in Red Light Districts.

The "Blue Book," as the preface reproduced on this page informs us, was an essential guide to The District. Miss Josie Arlington's, the dining room of which is shown above, and Miss Lulu White's, described on the facing page, were among the fanciest mansions. The photograph shows Miss White's Mahogany Hall just before it was torn down in the late 1940s.

MISS LULU WHITE

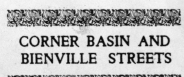

CORNER BASIN AND
BIENVILLE STREETS

Nowhere in this country will you find a more popular personage than Madame White, who is noted as being the handsomest octoroon in America, and aside from her beauty, she has the distinction of possessing the largest collection of diamonds, pearls, and other rare gems in this part of the country.

To see her at night, is like witnessing the electrical display on the Cascade, at the late St. Louis Exposition.

Aside from her handsome women, her mansion possesses some of the most costly oil paintings in the Southern country. Her mirror-parlor is also a dream.

There's always something new at Lulu White's that will interest you. ''Good time'' is her motto.

There are always ten entertainers, who recently arrived from the ''East,'' some being well known to the ''profession,'' who get paid to do nothing but sing and dance.

PHONES MAIN 1102 AND 1331.

Lulu White.

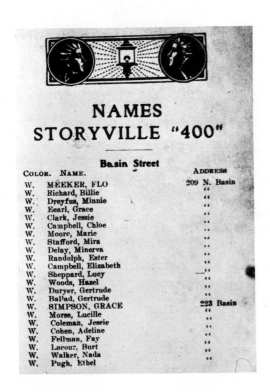

NAMES
STORYVILLE "400"

Basin Street

COLOR.	NAME.	ADDRESS
W.	MEEKER, FLO	209 N. Basin
W.	Richard, Billie	''
W.	Dreyfus, Minnie	''
W.	Eearl, Grace	''
W.	Clark, Jessie	''
W.	Campbell, Chloe	''
W.	Moore, Marie	''
W.	Stafford, Mira	''
W.	Delay, Minerva	''
W.	Randolph, Ester	''
W.	Campbell, Elizabeth	''
W.	Sheppard, Lucy	''
W.	Woods, Hazel	''
W.	Duryer, Gertrude	''
W.	Ballad, Gertrude	''
W.	SIMPSON, GRACE	223 Basin
W.	Morse, Lucille	''
W.	Coleman, Jessie	''
W.	Cohen, Adeline	''
W.	Fellman, Fay	''
W.	Lacour, Burt	''
W.	Walker, Nada	''
W.	Pugh, Ethel	''

Tom Anderson's cafe was a major musical center of Storyville, located at Basin and Iberville Streets, just a few doors from Mahogany Hall—indicated in top photograph by an arrow. In the band there, in this pre-1915 photo, were Manuel Perez and such to-be-heard-again names as Paul Barbarin *(left)*, Luis Russell *(center)*, Albert Nicholas *(right)*.

The Onward Brass Band, ready to parade, about 1913. The very busy Manuel Perez is at the left; third from left is Peter Bocage (who can also be seen as the violinist-leader of the Superior Band on page 7); next to him is Lorenzo Tio, Jr., teacher of many great clarinetists.

This dim photo is all that remains of the Tuxedo Band, led by cornetist Oscar "Papa" Celestin and including three who were to be important names in Chicago days: Jimmy Noone (rear, left), bassist John Lindsay (rear, right), banjoist Johnny St. Cyr (front, right).

It should be clear that lineups shifted constantly, and daytime jobs could be quite separate from night. Here is Papa Celestin (second from right) in the brass band led by Henry Allen, Sr. (right), which had neighboring Algiers, La., as its home base.

Buddy Petit (*center*) was "one of the greatest hot cornets that ever lived," according to Jelly Roll Morton, but he never went North, and so has survived only as a dim name. The very young clarinetist in his 1920 band was Edmond Hall.

Zue Robertson was credited by many with setting the style for all who followed on the slide trombone, but he was a "rambler" and "irresponsible," which is probably why lasting fame eluded him. At the left he is in the uniform of a Wild West Show band with which he played in about 1917; at the right, with his sister and brother-in-law, year unknown, in Norfolk, Virginia.

These bands, which probably featured a smoother, "Creole" vein of music, made some pioneering impressions on the outside world. At the top: Manuel Perez' 1915 band, probably the first to fill a regular dance job in Chicago. Below them is the orchestra led by violinist Armand J. Piron, among the very first Negro groups to record for a major company (Victor, in 1923). Piron had Peter Bocage *(left)* on trumpet; Louis "Old Man" Cotrelle, who taught many of the early drummers, is in both groups, and so is clarinetist Lorenzo Tio, Jr. *(right in Perez photo; fifth from left with Piron).*

Freddie Keppard was among the very great New Orleans horns, with matchless range and inventiveness. With Adie Venson, trombone, and George Baquet, clarinet, he made up the Original Creole Orchestra front line. Bill Johnson was on bass; seated *(left to right)* are drummer Dink Johnson; Jimmie Palao, violin; Norwood Williams, guitar. First to make extended tours, in vaudeville, they were in Chicago, New York, California, between 1913 and 1918. The snapshots show Keppard in band uniform and with young Sidney Bechet *(standing)*.

14

Joe Oliver was called "King," no empty title in New Orleans. His Creole Jazz Band (above), greatest of traditional jazz groups, was not formed until he reached Chicago, but only pianist Lil Hardin was not New Orleans-bred. *Left to right:* Baby Dodds, drums; Honore Dutray, trombone; Oliver *(seated);* Bill Johnson, bass and banjo; Louis Armstrong, second cornet; Johnny Dodds, clarinet. The picture of Oliver below was taken on Canal Street. The "Big 25," known earlier as Pete Lala's, was Storyville's foremost musicians' hangout; Oliver led a band there. This 1954 photo was taken shortly before it was torn down.

Many riverboats carried jazz up the Mississippi and along its tributaries—excursion steamers like the one shown below: S.S. *President* of the Streckfus line. Pianist Fate Marable (who also played the calliope) was their most noted bandleader. Below is a later picture of Marable; in the summer of 1918, the talented lineup he led had Baby Dodds on drums and his older brother Johnny on clarinet; Johnny St. Cyr, banjo; Pops Foster, bass; Bill Ridgeley, trombone; Dave Jones, mellophone. One trumpeter was Joe Howard; the other, next to Fate, may be young Louis Armstrong.

These two pictures, taken in the San Francisco area in the early 1920s, help to indicate that the dispersal of jazz from New Orleans came sooner and was more far-flung than many realize. Kid Ory, who was also to figure prominently in the Chicago picture in the mid-'20s, had gone to the West Coast before Storyville closed down. The band shown here, which had Mutt Carey on trumpet, played in Oakland. In the other photo, Ory *(left)* and bass-player Ed Garland are shown on the Oakland-San Francisco ferry in 1922. (In Chapter 17, Ory, Garland and Carey can be found together twenty-five years later.) There was actually considerable jazz activity in California: for a while in 1921, both King Oliver's band and Jelly Roll Morton were in Los Angeles. And from the early part of the century's second decade, bands had traveled through the South and Southwest; and several, as noted, had worked in Chicago. Jazz was beginning to find its way around in the world.

2

Original Dixieland One Step

THEY HAD learned the music of the Negroes in New Orleans, and they brought their "jass" to Chicago, New York, London, and the world at large. Thus to a vast number of people, for quite a long time, the kind of music the Original Dixieland Jazz Band played represented *all* of jazz.

Actually, the impression that this particular band was, in itself, a starting point is somewhat of an exaggeration. They were far from being the first jazz band, of course; were not even among the very first white bands, nor the first to bring the music out of New Orleans and up North. But they do have to their credit a couple of extremely important firsts: they were the first to make an impact on New York, and they made the initial jazz recordings, in 1917. Like many another group of their time, they went in for cowbells and other dubious "novelty" effects. Nevertheless, they were thoroughly authentic jazzmen, directly in the line of descent from the bands that first established the white jazz tradition.

It is "Papa" Jack Laine who stands as the founder of that tradition. He had organized his Reliance Brass Band as far back as 1892, and led a Ragtime Band before 1900. Although clearly influenced by what men like Buddy Bolden were creating at that time, Laine's music was distinctively that of the marching bands and of ragtime. In the heavily musical atmosphere of New Orleans at the turn of the century, there developed several bands led, or at least organized, by Laine. Later, his son and various alumni of his groups became bandleaders. Youngsters such as George Brunies and Nick LaRocca played within the Laine framework, and also listened eagerly (as no one who cared for this kind of music

could help doing) to what the Negroes were playing through the streets of the city and in the cabarets of Storyville. Thus the form of jazz they evolved was both directly and indirectly influenced by the mainstream of music in their home town: directly through what they absorbed themselves; indirectly through the slightly earlier synthesis that Laine had made. What emerged was something that was both their own and quite close to the New Orleans Negro sound: rough, unwritten, played largely in an ensemble style (solos were a great rarity in those days).

With two major exceptions, however, these young white bands were doomed to be overshadowed by others: in the history of jazz the emphasis is on the Negro groups in New Orleans and, in the Chicago period that followed, on both the Negroes who moved northward and the young Chicagoans who adopted jazz. Thus most of these early Dixielanders are today only vaguely remembered names. But those two exceptions are of extreme importance. One was the previously mentioned Original Dixieland Jazz Band, which left a permanent mark on New York jazz and on the style that today is still known under the general name of Dixieland. The second was the slightly younger New Orleans Rhythm Kings. Only its nucleus (including young George Brunies) was New Orleans-bred, but it was strictly in the original tradition, and almost from the moment it was formed in Chicago, in the very early '20s, exerted a deep influence on the young generation of jazzmen in that city.

And let it also be noted that of all jazz bands in any era, only these two—the ODJB and the NORK—ever achieved the great American hallmark of popularity: to be completely identifiable by initials only.

The *original* Original Dixieland Jazz Band.   19

Even for the white musicians, New Orleans was a city of parades and street bands. Jack Laine is shown, *facing left* and holding kettle drum, on Mardi Gras day in 1903. In the lower photograph, taken at the resort area known as the West End, are Abbie Brunies, Charlie Cordilla and Emil Lacoume, nicknamed "Stale Bread," who played zither, piano, banjo and guitar, and led various "spasm" bands consisting of such home-made instruments as cheese-box banjo and soap-box guitar.

George Brunies was listening to the music of Storyville and playing it almost before he was out of short pants. In these photos, taken in about 1917, he must be seventeen but looks even younger and more fresh-faced. The band is Albert "Baby" Laine's; he is the cornetist (note the attached tin-can mute) and his father is the drummer. Charlie Cordilla is on clarinet; Herman Ragas, bass; Jules Reiner, piano. The non-playing picture shows the strong resemblance between the two Laines (leaning on opposite sides of the bench).

The leaders of these two bands are among the unsung Dixieland pioneers. Alcide "Yellow" Nunez, Louisiana Five clarinetist, first came North with the Original Dixieland Jazz Band (he is in the photograph on page 18), but was traded to Tom Brown's band before the ODJB recorded. As for Brown, shown here with his 1921 Dixieland Band, the trombonist had brought the first white band to Chicago in 1915—and, when local musicians tried to smear them by calling them a "jass" band (the word had strictly red-light district meanings, according to the story), turned the term into a crowd-pulling asset by billing his group as "Brown's Dixieland Jass Band."

Three varied photos of the Original Dixieland Jazz Band, showing their several fancy mutes and drummer Tony Sbarbaro's giant kazoo *(center picture)*. Only the top photo shows the band that made the historic first jazz recordings *(left to right)*: Sbarbaro (later changed to Spargo), Eddie Edwards, Nick LaRocca, Larry Shields (who had come from Brown's band in exchange for Nunez), Henry Ragas. Before the group left for its sensational tour of England, Ragas died, and J. Russell Robinson *(center and bottom photos)* took his place. Edwards, declining to go to Europe, was replaced by trombonist Emil Christian, shown in the bottom picture, taken in London in 1919.

One early Dixieland group, highly rated in its day and now unremembered, was led by pianist Norman Brownlee. The cornetist in this band, who also played on the riverboats, is Emmett Hardy, a dim and legendary figure (he never recorded, and died at 22) who is reputed to have influenced Bix Beiderbecke.

Three early views of clarinetist Tony Parenti, the only New Orleans Dixieland veteran still fully active in New York in the mid-1960s. Parenti is shown in 1911, aged about ten; and with two early local bands. He is at the right in the gay photo of the five-man Johnny De Droit band, another now forgotten early group; in the bottom picture, Parenti stands with folded hands amid the band he led on the be-draped stand at the LaVida Club on Burgundy Street, in 1924.

A band that took the music afield: the New Orleans Rhythm Masters, at the Somerset Club in San Antonio, Texas, in October, 1926. Terry Shand is the pianist, Sidney Arodin the clarinetist, Charlie Cordilla, the ex-Laine bandsman, on saxophone. The young trombone player is local Texas talent: Jack Teagarden.

Cordilla *(sixth from left),* tuba player Chink Martin, and Arodin *(at Martin's left)* went even further afield with the New Orleans Swing Kings, photographed at a Catskill Mountains (New York) resort in 1930. Sidney Arodin was one of the very few to play with both white and Negro groups in New Orleans.

The Halfway House Orchestra led by trumpeter Abbie Brunies had such sound members as Charlie Cordilla *(left)* and drummer Monk Hazel, but is remembered largely as the last group with which Leon Rappolo played after leaving the New Orleans Rhythm Kings and before entering the sanitarium he never left. The brilliant clarinetist (playing alto sax here) left as his legacy the several graceful, haunting solos on his NORK records. (This picture bears out the story that he wore white socks with his tuxedo, but that the photographer blacked them in on the standard band photo.)

Recording Information of Wax No. 11352
11352A
11352B

Date Recorded 3-12-23   By   E C A Wickemeyer   Richmond, Ind.

Subject "SWEET LOVIN' MAN"

By New Orleans Rhythm Kings, Formerly Accompanied by
Friar's Society Orchestra

Composed by   Music by   Hardin-Melrose

Words by   Hardin-Melrose   Published by   Melrose Brothers, Chicago

Copyright   19   Royalties

Recording Expense

Wax Shipped   Trunk No.   Via

Suggest Using in   Supplement

Remarks

The Friars Society Orchestra, in Chicago, 1922: Ben Pollack *(rear)* is the drummer; the others *(left to right)* are George Brunies, Paul Mares, Leon Rappolo, Elmer Schoebel, Jack Pettis, Lew Black, Steve Brown.

Paul Mares.

The influence of two white New Orleans groups was, as has been noted, indeed great: the ODJB giving the New York jazz tradition its impetus, and the NORK impressing the young Chicago crowd, with far-reaching results, with the recordings they made for the Gennett label. (The card on the facing page is from one of those sessions; by 1923 they had dropped their first band name, derived from the Friar's Inn, where they played.) Rather strangely, few of these New Orleans men remained on the active jazz scene. George Brunies is the really notable exception (Ben Pollack was a native Chicagoan); most of the others drifted back home by the '20s, continuing to play there, but making no further contribution to the main stream of jazz.

3

Stockyard Strut

WHEN STORYVILLE closed down, it was time for almost everyone to move up-river, to Chicago, which was just about as wide-open a town, with just about as many night spots that could use good jazz bands. And being a Northern town, it was undoubtedly, all things considered, a better place for a Negro musician to live.

It wasn't quite that simple and direct, of course; things never are. It's true enough that New Orleans' red-light district was closed down completely and suddenly during World War I, following War and Navy Department orders. November 12, 1917, was its final day. (The upshot was that the houses moved, a bit more quietly, into other parts of the city, while the musicians who had worked at the rip-roaring joints were without places in which to play.) A partial exodus had begun before this, with bands traveling into Texas and as far as California, and with the riverboats carrying jazz up to St. Louis and Kansas City. Some adventurous souls had already explored Chicago, as noted in the first chapter. On the other hand, there were musicians who were to choose not to leave New Orleans at all. But on the whole the closing of Storyville meant a dispersal of jazz, and Chicago met the requirements as its new home. Straight up the Mississippi from New Orleans, it had a growing Negro population. Good-paying jobs attracted Southern workers to its stockyards and the outlying steel mills. With the enactment of Prohibition, the Windy City became the home port for the major bootleggers and thus a center of a rough, flourishing night life.

All that remains today of the original music of New Orleans is, basically, the jazz played in Chicago in the '20s. This seeming paradox is easily explained: in the Southern city there had been no recording of jazz; now, in Chicago, many companies, large and small, were taking it down, just as clubs and dance halls and theaters of all descriptions were employing jazz musicians regularly—all of this activity bringing about what is generally described as a "Golden Age" of jazz. King Oliver's Creole Jazz Band, which scored the first great success in Chicago, was faithful to the early ensemble-jazz tradition, but the music as a whole was gradually undergoing a fundamental change. For one thing, jazz here was strictly a night-life music: parades and funerals were of the past. As the bands played for a different audience (often enough, a white audience), the tight-knit early pattern altered. There were varying paths for the music to follow. In the larger clubs and the vaudeville theaters, a much smoother style developed, the bands increasing their size and often making at least partial use of written arrangements. Among those who played almost exclusively for Negro audiences in the small, tough dives on the South Side that were probably not too different from New Orleans bars, there evolved a loose-jointed, rhythmic music. It was played by three- and four-man groups, often including such odd instruments as washboard or kazoo. The key figure of this style was the fluid-toned, amazingly versatile clarinetist, Johnny Dodds.

But no matter in what direction the movement might be, traditional jazz was changing, and the Chicago era became the first great period of the solo virtuoso: Louis Armstrong, Johnny Dodds, Jimmy Noone, Earl Hines, and many others, setting a pattern that was forever after the norm in jazz.

King Oliver's Creole Jazz Band.

Joe Oliver quickly established himself in Chicago, playing at the Royal Gardens, Dreamland, the Pekin, although not yet with exactly the classic Creole Band personnel. The posed, in-costume photo above was taken in San Francisco, where they journeyed in 1921 for a dance-hall job, with Johnny Dodds, Honore Dutrey, Lil Hardin, but with Minor Hall as drummer and Ed Garland on bass. They soon returned to Chicago, to the Lincoln Gardens (which was the Royal Gardens, repainted and renamed), and to tuxedos.

Recording Information of Wax No. 11635
11635A
11635B
11635C

Date Recorded 10-5-23   By E.C.A. Wickemeyer Richmond, Ind.

Subject "ZULUS BALL"

By King Oliver & his Creole Jazz Band Accompanied by

Composed by   Music by Oliver - Robinson

Words by Oliver - Robinson   Published by Melrose.

Copyright   19   Royalties

Recording Expense

Wax Shipped   Trunk No.   Via

Suggest Using in   Supplement

Remarks

The Gennett recording card is proof of the existence of the incredibly rare *Zulu's Ball.* By 1923, Oliver having sent for Louis Armstrong, the lineup was set as in the upper photo on page 15: Baby Dodds, Dutrey, Oliver, Bill Johnson, Armstrong, Johnny Dodds, Lil Hardin. But the following year, for still-debated reasons, dissension ripped the band apart. In the photo below, Louis and Lil remain; those with them include saxophonists Buster Bailey *(third from left)* and Rudy Jackson *(right),* and a bespectacled Zue Robertson on trombone.

31

Armstrong left Oliver later in 1924, and the King sought to reorganize. But on Christmas Eve, his new opening night, the Lincoln Gardens was gutted by fire, and Oliver spent a few unhappy months featured with Dave Peyton's Symphonic Syncopators. By March, 1925, however, he had succeeded Peyton at the Plantation Cafe with his new Dixie Syncopators, a talented group that included Bud Scott, banjo; Paul Barbarin, drums; Luis Russell, piano; Bob Schoffner as second trumpet; and a young reed section of (*left to right*) Darnell Howard, Albert Nicholas, Barney Bigard.

Oliver with Peyton's Symphonic Syncopators.

Among the things that Louis and Lil (by then Mr. and Mrs. Armstrong) went on to were the sensational Hot Five recording sessions, with *(from the left)* banjoist Johnny St. Cyr, Kid Ory, Johnny Dodds.

A later small band found Lil teamed with still another great horn, huge Freddie Keppard, in a small group that played in the Illinois area in 1928.

Many New Orleans musicians found their way to Chicago before the main wave, as already noted. Among the first were these. Above, on the stage of a South Side theater in 1915 and below, at the De Luxe Cafe slightly later, are "Sugar Johnny," known as an "erratic but sensational" cornetist, and the equally legendary Roy Palmer, trombone, and Lawrence Duhé, clarinet. With them at the De Luxe were bassist Wellman Braud, and Lil Hardin (obscured by an imperfection in the print), newly arrived from Memphis.

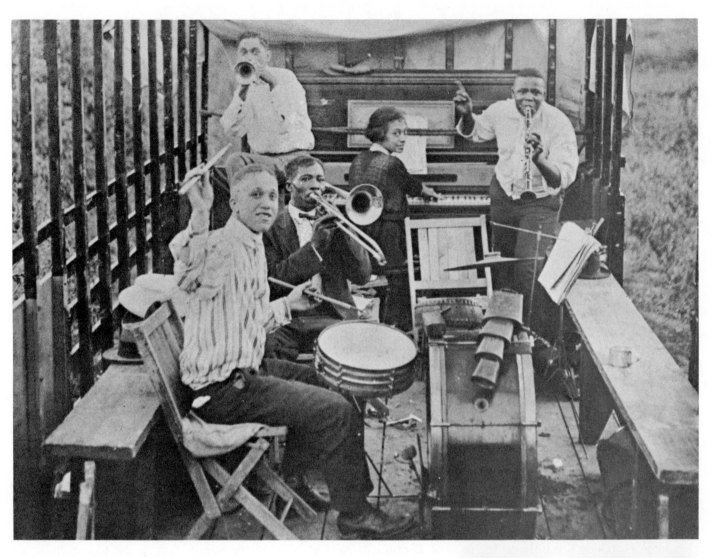

The riverboats made St. Louis one of their important
stops en route, and thus rate credit for establishing a
"school" that funnelled jazz into Chicago and elsewhere.
In the top picture, dating to the very early '20s, the
young clarinetist is Gene Sedric and the girl at the piano
is probably Marge Creath, sister of Charlie Creath—who
led a noted St. Louis band of this period.

Below is a rare picture of the little-known Ike Rodgers,
a crude trombonist (said to be able to play "only two
notes") who made some remarkable late-'20s records in
Chicago.

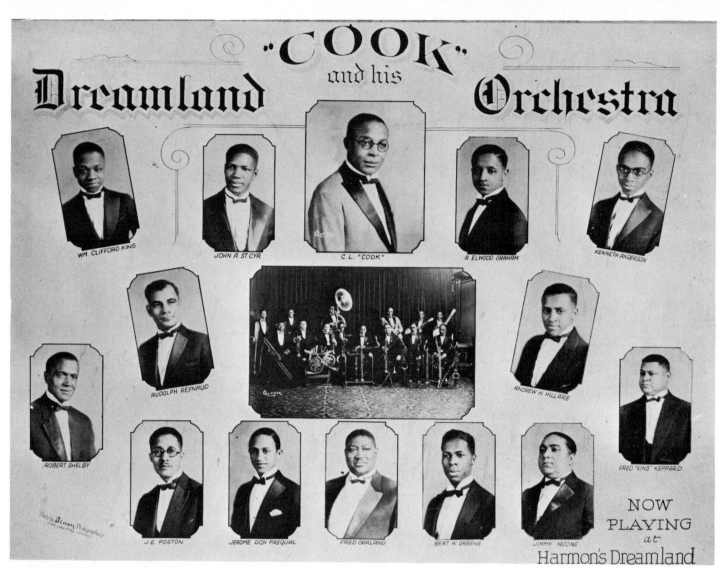

"COOK" and his
Dreamland Orchestra

WM. CLIFFORD KING — JOHN A. ST CYR — C.L. "COOK" — R. ELWOOD GRAHAM — KENNETH ANDERSON

RUDOLPH REYNAUD — ANDREW H. HILLAIRE

ROBERT SHELBY — FRED "KING" KEPPARD

J.E. POSTON — JEROME DON PASQUAL — FRED GARLAND — BERT W. GREENE — JIMMY NOONE

NOW PLAYING at Harmon's Dreamland

Doc Cook's orchestra was large for its day (fourteen men), but it boasted two of the true New Orleans giants: Freddie Keppard and clarinetist Jimmy Noone, as well as Johnny St. Cyr on banjo and drummer Andrew Hilaire, to give it some highly effective moments. By 1923 Keppard was willing to record; in 1916 he had declined a Victor offer that would have given his Creole Band the honor that instead went to the ODJB, saying he didn't want his "stuff on records for everyone to steal."

Jazz bands found no shortage of clubs as the '20s rolled along. Drummer Ollie Powers' Harmony Syncopators were at the Dreamland in 1923. (Keppard, and later Armstrong, played briefly with this group.)

The Moulin Rouge was another booming night spot, featuring a band led by trumpeter Jimmy Wade, with Teddy Weatherford (who later spent most of his career in India!) on piano.

Often sharing the bandstand at the Moulin Rouge was the Wonder Orchestra of Clarence Jones, reputedly a pianist and arranger far in advance of his times.

CARROLL DICKERSON ORCHESTRA.

F. HALL.　J. HALL.　M. CARR.　D. BROW..

H. DUTREY.　W. H. HIGHTOWER　E. HINES.　C. IRWIN.

A. DOMINIQUE　CARROLL DICKERSON.　E. BROWN.

With the personnel of many early bands now in doubt or dispute, one can be thankful for this advertising card that makes it clear that Carroll Dickerson toured the Pantages vaudeville circuit with a band including Earl Hines on piano, trumpeters Willie Hightower and Natty Dominique, trombonist Honore Dutrey and drummer Tubby Hall.

Without clues like that on the top photo on this page, it can only be noted that this picture of a late-'20s Doc Cook band shows the remarkable bandstand decor at White City, a noted South Side amusement park.

The huge Tiny Parham was a leading figure on the South Side scene. A pianist, he led well-schooled bands that appeared in the larger night clubs and at vaudeville theaters.

Erskine Tate's Vendome Theater Orchestra, in one of the busy-busy pictures that, for unknown reasons, were all the rage when bands visited photographers' studios in the '20s. An early (probably 1921) photo of a group that was the foremost theater-pit band of the period. At the right, since time brings changes, is the Vendome Theater in the process of being torn down, in 1949.

Trumpeter Willie Hightower (fourth from left) made a few quite rare recordings with his own Night Hawks band, making the leadership of this group a slight puzzle (unless the title ran in the family). In the band are New Orleans trombonist John Lindsay (left); and Bert Cobb, who also played tuba with Oliver's Dixie Syncopators.

Large bands became the order of the day in the later '20s, and the excess of instruments on these bandstands indicates how much "doubling" a musician was expected to do. The top photo is of Junie C. Cobb's band, at the Club Metropole in 1929; Cobb himself could play trumpet, clarinet, alto sax and banjo. Below them is the Hugh Swift Orchestra, successful in 1927, but long-forgotten now.

Albert Wynn, who had played trombone behind blues singer Ma Rainey in the early '20s, led this band—which traveled as far as Paris.

Still another notable larger band was Sammy Stewart's. In 1925 it was distinguished by the presence of drummer Big Sid Catlett, towering in the rear, and pianist Alec Hill, at Catlett's right. The leader wears the raccoon coat.

Frankie "Half Pint" Jaxon, a leading vaudeville performer with considerable jazz feeling, worked, in the mid-'20s, with this group that included trumpeter Bob Schoffner and drummer Tubby Hall.

Tiny Parham.

"Mr. Freddie" Shayne.

Richard M. Jones.

Jesse Crump.

In a period abounding with talented piano players, these were certainly among the best. Frank Melrose, brother of the music-publishing Melroses, studied with Jelly Roll Morton, recorded as "Kansas City Frank," and could hold his own with any of the South Siders.

Lovie Austin.

Frank Melrose.

Jimmy Bertrand.

Johnny Dodds.

Herb Morand.

Lee Collins.

The card at the top of the page is from a Jimmy Blythe recording session for the Champion label, with Jimmy Bertrand probably on washboard. Pianist Blythe, who died in 1930, was, along with the versatile Johnny Dodds, in the forefront of the "South Side style," which meant small-band recordings and jobs at small, rough clubs along with trumpet men like Collins, Morand, Natty Dominique.

Earl Hines came out of Pittsburgh in the mid-'20s, played with Louis Armstrong at the Sunset Cafe and on several notable record dates, and quickly developed into an outstanding and style-setting pianist. He formed this band to play at the opening of the Grand Terrace Ballroom in 1928, and remained an important bandleader throughout the Swing Era and beyond. Two great clarinetists flank Hines here: Omer Simeon is on his right, Darnell Howard on his left.

The Dodds brothers, trumpeter Natty Dominique, Lil Hardin Armstrong, in 1939.

The graceful and fluid-toned Jimmy Noone, one of the great New Orleans clarinetists, remained almost entirely faithful to the small-band style, making this 1930s photo of a twelve-piece Noone band a rarity.

Left to right: Little Brother Montgomery, Lonnie Johnson, John Lindsay (he could play both bass and trombone), Tubby Hall, Darnell Howard, Lee Collins, Preston Jackson, at a latter-day concert.

This is the way the Chicago chapter must end: with Johnny Dodds as he was briefly brought out of obscurity a year before his death in 1940; with Jimmie Noone leading a big band; with a gang of "old-timers" presenting an occasional concert. Jazz goes on in Chicago still, but first the Depression and then changing public taste made it a far cry from the triumphal early days of Oliver and Keppard and Armstrong.

est wishes to
Howard
from
Louis Armstrong

4

Dippermouth

No DOUBT about it, Louis Armstrong has played more jazz than any other man. It seems quite safe to state that no one else who plays his kind of music ever has been (or ever will be) nearly so good as the man they call "Satchmo" for anything like so long. His career bridges just about the whole history of jazz to date, and for much more than half his life he has been billed as "The World's Greatest Trumpeter." And it would be difficult indeed to find anyone unwilling to grant that the billing has been an accurate one, at least for a very substantial portion of the time.

It is, actually, the length of time that he has been near or at the top of the heap that complicates matters somewhat when it comes to evaluating Louis. There have been, you must say, several different Louis Armstrongs—all of them remarkable performers, but not the same at all. There is a boy learning to play the cornet in what amounted to a reform school in New Orleans and then, while still in his 'teens, working in Storyville and on the riverboats. There's a young man invited into the big time, asked to join the band of his idol and early teacher, Joe Oliver, in Chicago. Then the protégé quickly overshadows King Joe and, in a swift montage of ever-increasing success, there is the young star of many classic recording dates, a bandleader, a celebrity in Chicago, New York, Hollywood, England, France—any place you care to name. He becomes a great virtuoso, hitting and holding those dazzling high notes, dominating a whole generation of trumpet men (both the many who try to imitate him and the few who try to avoid doing so). In the most recent decades there is Louis Armstrong the showman, the entertainer, playing, singing and clowning all at the same time, and—wonder of wonders—creating a top record hit in his sixties.

Simply by changing from a rough, driving New Orleans horn to a master showman, Louis has inevitably disappointed some who preferred him at one earlier point or another. But, in changing, he has become synonymous with jazz to millions of people. Many of these (who probably have never of their own free will listened to any jazz other than his) identify the music only with the warmth and appeal of his trumpet sound, his raspy voice, his personality—which is an accomplishment not to be taken lightly.

Louis has never been taken lightly by those who have heard him or have known him. Even circumstance seems on his side, as in the case of his impossible-to-disregard birthdate: July 4, 1900. He has always been looked upon by fellow musicians with a mixture of awe, respect and love, from the earliest New Orleans and Chicago days. He was no more than seventeen when Oliver left Storyville, but it was he who was chosen to take the King's place in a Kid Ory band; and the series of affectionate nicknames he has had—Kid Louis, Dippermouth, Satchmo—were all given him by the musicians he worked with. It's easy enough to explain his initial success: he was simply the *best*, with a rich, full sound, a tone and fire and beauty that have never been surpassed. But the truly remarkable achievement, which can best be phrased as a question, is this: How many men, in any field and any period of time, have, like Louis, been accepted with equal admiration both by their fellow professionals and by the public at large?

In the picture of the "Colored Waif's Home" band, the arrow points to young Louis, aged about eleven, in the middle of the top row. Sent to the home after shooting off a pistol in the street during a New Year's celebration, he reputedly learned to play on the bugle and cornet shown here. In the formal studio portrait, solemn, 'teen-aged Louis poses with his mother and his sister Beatrice.

48

One of the first jobs to take young Louis away from New Orleans was with a Fate Marable band. On the riverboat S. S. *Capital*, in 1919, his co-workers included Johhny St. Cyr and Baby Dodds.

Then, in 1923, came the telegram from King Oliver, who had been "like a father" in New Orleans. One more photo of the Creole Band (most people will agree that there couldn't be too many views of this remarkable group), this time one of those jazzed-up poses, with Louis handling a slide trumpet he probably never played.

To Kid Muggsy
Shown
Louis Armstrong

GENERAL PHONOGRAPH CORPORATION

Record Laboratory

9484-a

DATE *Nov 12, 1925*

Recorded by *D*

Laboratory No.   Size *10"*

Catalogue No. *8320-B*

Coupled with *9535-a*

Special Catalogue No. *June 5 1926*

Selection *My Heart*

By *Louis Armstrong and His Hot Five*   Accompanied by

Composed by *Lillian Armstrong*

From

Publisher *Consolidated Music Pub. House*   Copyright *76*   19

Address *227 W. Washington St, Chicago, Ill*

I sent contract 5-24-26

Remarks *Race*

Made in Chicago Ill.   *2 cent white — 20 5/8*

An Okeh recording card from a Hot Five session.

In addition to recording, Satchmo managed to hold down two jobs, one at the Dreamland Cafe, the other with Erskine Tate's band (shown here) at the Vendome Theater. It was with this band, which included Jimmy Bertrand on drums, that Louis switched from cornet to the richer-sounding trumpet. He also began doing on-stage specialties, including vocals.

When Louis left Oliver, there was a brief stay with Fletcher Henderson in New York, and then back to Chicago, where probably the most lastingly important work he did was to make his Hot Five recordings, with St. Cyr, Johnny Dodds, Ory, and his wife.

At the Sunset Cafe, owned by Joe Glaser (Louis' manager to-day), he began his career as bandleader, in 1927. As the photo suggests, Earl Hines (left) did much of the actual leading. Honore Dutrey is on trombone; Tubby Hall, the drummer.

Through much of the '30s, the band Louis fronted amid fancy stage settings was that of pianist Luis Russell. Pops Foster is the bass player; Jimmy Archey is the trombonist on the right.

Armstrong's first return to New Orleans was with this band, which had made the hugely successful recording of *Sleepy Time Down South*. This is the Suburban Gardens, in 1931; Tubby Hall is on drums; John Lindsay, bass; Preston Jackson, trombone.

The public view of Louis in the '30s: two publicity photos (note the billing as "World's Greatest Trumpeter"; Oliver had never reached more than "World's Greatest Jazz Cornetist"); a still from the movie "Artists and Models"; and the marquee of Loew's State, in New York, 1937.

A more personal view. In the left-hand top picture, Louis with his third wife, Alpha, in Paris in 1934; next to it, with his present wife, Lucille, in 1950. Below, at the left, with his old friend of New Orleans days, drummer Zutty Singleton, in California in 1946. At the right, outside the Armstrong home (Long Island, New York) in 1950.

54

Both before and after World War II, there were tours of Europe. Shown with Louis here is the great French guitarist, Django Reinhardt.

Armstrong at his ease with some professional associates: with trumpeters Lee Castle, Joe Thomas, Bobby Hackett, all self-confessed admirers; with singer Billie Holiday; relaxed, but at work, while rehearsing for a 1940s Carnegie Hall concert. The clarinetist is Edmond Hall.

By the end of the '40s, Louis had given up big bands—but this was by no means a sign of lessening activity. He has been on the road almost constantly ever since, with small groups. (The first such unit is shown above; it included Jack Teagarden, Barney Bigard, and drummer Sid Catlett, and also had his sidekick of the '20s, Earl Hines, on piano.) And his broad definition of the "road" has included all continents, as more and more of the world's population has been able to see and hear "Ambassador Satch." His recording activities, after a rather barren period combining him with vocal groups and lush arrangements, suddenly reverted to a jazz-tinged leanness and unprecedented popular success: in the late '50s with "Mack the Knife" and in '64 with an incredibly best-selling "Hello, Dolly." Reaching the top of the sales list in direct competition with such acts as The Beatles was surely a good way for Louis to demonstrate his unwillingness to ever stop swinging.

5

Mr. Jelly Lord

JELLY ROLL MORTON claimed to have "created jazz in 1901" (or to have "discovered" it, or "originated" it— Morton was a frequent talker on the grand scale, and the stories varied) and, in a way, he wasn't too far from the truth. For the significant thing to remember about Jelly Roll is that he was a genius. He was also a braggart, a colorful and opinionated egocentric— but he was unquestionably that rarity among boasters, a man who could back up his words with his accomplishments.

Ferdinand Joseph Morton (the family name apparently had originally been the French "La Menthe") was born in New Orleans about 1885. At a very early age he was playing piano in the dives of the Storyville district and, despite his youth, was a major and influential figure. Thus he was certainly among those who had an important role in shaping (or "creating") the new music. Of course, he could also have meant that he "developed" jazz, which would tie in with another widely-quoted Morton boast, that "all styles are Jelly Roll style." This sweeping remark can be approached in at least two ways. For one, Morton was thoroughly familiar, from childhood on, with just about all the threads of the musical pattern of his home town. He heard and played the blues, the stomps and ragtime on the streets and in the honky-tonks, and also absorbed French and Spanish influences. All this he made his own, so that when as a solo pianist or as leader and driving force of a band, he displayed his remarkable mastery of the combined product, "all styles" were present and all were stamped with his distinctive touch. On the other hand, the impact of his first Red Hot Peppers band recordings in the mid-1920s was so sweeping, and so many other bands showed clear evidence of having been influenced by his work, that there was a reasonable basis for his feeling that virtually everyone was adopting a "Jelly Roll style."

Morton himself, however, would not have appreciated any such equivocal explanations of his blunt, uncompromising statements. He meant what he said, and he felt that for those who would listen to it, his music supported him fully. Actually, it was some time before very many people would listen. He did considerable wandering, first through the South, then in California and the Midwest. It was not until 1926, when he was about forty years old, that he really came into his own, through the first Red Hot Peppers records. For the next several years, in Chicago and in New York, he remained on top, but lean years came later. The changing jazz styles of the post-1930 period edged him out of public favor, and Jelly (who wore a diamond in his stickpin and another in his tooth, and reputedly carried a thousand dollar bill with which to convince anyone who might doubt that he was doing well) was no man to conserve his assets. In 1938 he recorded an impressive documentary for the Library of Congress, singing, playing and talking his own life story and the story of early jazz in typically broad and colorful terms, and this brought him some attention. But his health had begun to fail; he continued to feel, bitterly, that he was under-appreciated; and in 1941 he died in a Los Angeles hospital.

Now that the man—just about the most flamboyant and exasperating personality imaginable—is gone, it is possible to evaluate his contributions to jazz more objectively. Now it can calmly be noted that Jelly Roll Morton, as a pianist, arranger, composer, and an organizer and leader of jazz bands, was a creator whose talents were of awesome and unique stature.

Jelly Roll Morton at a 1940 recording session.

A rare sample of Jelly Roll's handwriting, and an even rarer admission. Contrary to all his public expressions is this frank comment, in a letter to his close friend, Roy J. Carew, that it was a feeling of inferiority to other New Orleans pianists that led him to devise a non-ragtime style of playing.

Two rare youthful snapshots of Morton: in 1902, aged seventeen; and a few years later, with his wife, Anita Gonzales Morton.

"Ferd (Jelly Roll) Morton"—which is how he autographed this picture—in Chicago. This may date from
the early '20s, when he made his first records, including,
on one June day in 1924, no fewer than twenty master
recordings of piano solos for the Gennett company.

Address:- c/o Melrose Music Co., 177 No.State St., Chicago, Ill.
Records by: JELLY-ROLL MORTON'S RED HOT PEPPERS (Colored)

3 continued

Marking	Letter	Pitch	Serial No.	Matrix No.	Selection, Composer, Publisher, Copyright, Etc. (FM-HG)	Wax.	Rec.	F.Cur.	Level	Amp. Set	Eqlzr.	Fil.
					Chicago----Webster Hotel-December,16th.1926. Instr:-2 Violins-Cornet-Trombone-Clarinet-Banjo-St.Bass Piano & Trapman.							
P	BVE 100		37254	1	Someday Sweetheart -- Blues	55-135R	24	.7	H-4-5	6	On	.20
M	BVE 100		37254	2	Comp. Spikes & Spikes (John & Benjamin)	55-158	"	"	H-3-4	4	"	16
H30	BVE 100		37254	3	Pub. & Copyr., Melrose Bros., Music Co.,1924.	55-158	"	"	H-6-4	8	"	14
P	BVE 96		37255	1	Grandpa's Spells -- Stomp	55-145R	"	"	H-5-6	10	"	.16
H30	BVE 96		37255	2	Comp. Jelly Roll Morton, (date is)	55-122	"	"	H-4-5	8	"	"
M	BVE 96		37255	3	Pub. & Copyr., Melrose Bros.,Music Co.(1925, verbal)	55-122	"	"	H-3-4	6	"	14
H30	BVE 96		37256	1	Original Jelly Roll Blues	55-158	"	"	H-5-4	10	"	.16
M	BVE 96		37256	2	Comp. Jelly Roll Morton, Pub. & Copyr.,Melrose Bros.,1926 (Verbal by Mr.Melrose)	55-135R	"	"	H-5-3	8	"	14
P	BVE 100		37257	1	Doctor Jazz Stomp (Vocal by Jelly R.Morton)	55-150	"	"	H-4-3	6	"	.16
H30	BVE 100		37257	2	Comp. Joe Oliver,	55-121R	"	"	H-4-3	8	"	14
M	BVE 100		37257	3	Pub. & Copyr.,Melrose Bros.,1926 (Verbal by Mr. Melrose)	55-150	"	"	H-5-3	8	"	"
H30	BVE 100		37258	1	Cannon Ball Blues	55-150	"	"	H-5-3	8	"	.16
M	BVE 100		37258	2	Comp.Rider Bloom & Jelly R.Morton, Pub. & Copyr.,Melrose Bros.,1926 (Verbal by Mr. Melrose) Time 1:30 to 6:00 PM	55-158	"	"	H-4-3	6	"	14

In 1926, Morton made his first recordings for a major company. There were three sessions that Fall, from which emerged the first records to carry the Red Hot Peppers name. This group existed for recordings only; Jelly also had touring bands for a few years, using the same name but much less all-star line-ups. On 1927 recordings the personnel varied somewhat but was scarcely less impressive (the Dodds brothers were included among the newcomers). The Victor recording sheet pinpoints time, place, master numbers and instrumentation (Darnell Howard is believed to have been one of the violinists added for *Someday Sweetheart* only).

The lineup of the Red Hot Peppers, as pictured on these pages, is (*left to right in the above photo*): Andrew Hilaire, Kid Ory, George Mitchell, John Lindsay, Morton, Johnny St. Cyr, Omer Simeon. All were veterans; several still recall the intensive pre-recording rehearsals. The results surely were up to Jelly's rigid standards and are perhaps the finest of all recorded traditional jazz.

This pensive study, apparently taken at the same time as the action shot of the band on the preceding page, is the standard Morton picture. The photo on the facing page, with poised baton, is quite the opposite: an extremely rare item, taken when he had moved on to New York a year or so later.

A later, and somewhat less successful, Red Hot Peppers record date, in New York, in 1929. George Baquet is on clarinet *(standing behind the drums)*; Charlie Irvis on trombone *(standing next to tuba)*. Rather shocking to Morton fans is Jelly's non-playing baton-wielding pose. One Rod Rodriguez is at the piano.

"JELLY ROLL" MORTON
he originator of Jazz & stomps
AND HIS
RED HOT PEPPERS
MANAGEMENT

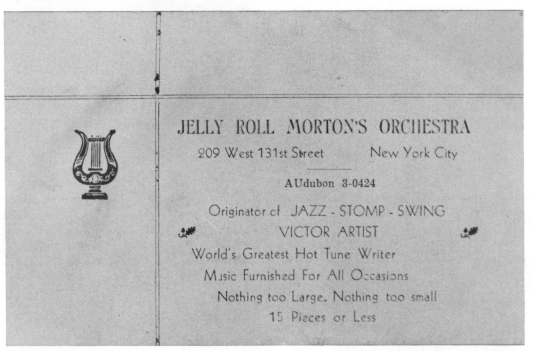

Some Morton memorabilia: shown in the photograph are some of the very few player-piano rolls made by Jelly Roll; the three business cards, from both Chicago and New York days, speak for themselves.

The portrait on the facing page, like the one on page 58, was made early in 1940, in New York, during his last record date—which, like his first, was for a small company.

6

Yonder Comes the Blues

MA RAINEY, Bessie Smith and all the backwoods singers whose names we'll never know—they understood what the blues was all about, its timeless and universal expression of pathos and irony and humor.

The blues dates back before the beginnings of jazz, and its origins are obscure beyond any hope of precise documentation, although it must have come into being somewhere in the deep rural South, sometime before the turn of this century. The concept of using roughly improvised song to tell about troubles or joys or just a generally rather bitter attitude towards money, sex and similar basic facts of life became standard among a Negro population recently freed from the restraints of slavery but still far short of equality. The first blues singers probably moaned a single strain on a single theme, singing without accompaniment or perhaps providing their own musical backing on a battered guitar. Soon enough, a definite pattern emerged: the words set into three-line stanzas that first stated the problem, then repeated it, finally carried it forward, with a hope or a curse or with resignation. Invariably, the blues made use of familiar objects and situations. The musical setting was always the simplest of melodic strains, never varying greatly and usually, though not inevitably, in a twelve-bar structure. The pattern became a rigid one, almost a ritual, but neither this rigidity nor its apparent simplicity has ever seemed to restrict the blues. Certainly some incredibly rich and moving singing and accompaniment and some highly effective folk-poetry belongs to this tradition, and instrumental blues have greatly enriched the mainstream of jazz.

Probably the first fully professional blues singers were the ragged men who wandered through the South, making a meager living on the streets and in rough bars by singing verses they invented, embellished or borrowed. The best-known and perhaps the best of them was Blind Lemon Jefferson. His work, unlike that of most of the others, has been preserved —he made a number of recordings in Chicago in the late 1920s—but virtually nothing is known of his life, and no photograph could be turned up for inclusion here.

The second phase of the early blues, generally called its "classic" period, was the era of the great female blues singers: women with throbbingly powerful voices, like Ma Rainey and the magnificent Bessie Smith, the several other unrelated Smith girls, Chippie Hill, and many others. They did not replace the earlier folk-blues tradition, but rather expanded it considerably into an entertainment form of tremendous impact and beauty. They performed in tent shows and on vaudeville stages throughout the South, then in Chicago and New York. With them the pattern of the blues grew somewhat less rough and more sophisticated. Piano and small-band accompaniment was the rule and in Chicago, where the blues singers were firmly a part of the "Golden Age" of the '20s, many of the great jazzmen worked and recorded with Ma and Bessie and the rest. In New York at this time and later, there was composer and publisher W. C. Handy, whose famous songs—*St. Louis Blues, Beale Street Blues* and the many others —were largely derived from folk-blues themes, and whose efforts helped make the blues a nationally known form.

The 1920s was the peak. Thereafter the blues tended to become watered down and intermingled with the products of Tin Pan Alley. But at that peak the blues, with its wit and sorrow and poetry and naked emotion, was, quite simply, great art.

Bessie Smith, an early portrait.

69

Gertrude Rainey, billed as "Madame" or "Ma" Rainey, was the first of the great "classic" blues singers, and very possibly the greatest, excepting only Bessie Smith, who was discovered and tutored by Ma. The eagle on the backdrop and the headdress were among her trademarks as she toured the Midwest and South in vaudeville and with her own Rabbits Foot Minstrels. In 1923, her youthful accompanists were Gabriel Washington, drums; Al Wynn, trombone; Dave Nelson (King Oliver's nephew), trumpet; Eddie Pollack, saxophone; Thomas A. Dorsey (now a gospel songwriter), piano.

Professio
Ma

Mamie Smith, who like Trixie, Laura and Clara Smith, was unrelated to Bessie or to any of the others, was nonetheless a notable blues singer, credited with making the first blues recording. Two members of her 1922 Jazz Hounds are worth a second look: trumpeter Bubber Miley and a sixteen-year-old saxophone player named Coleman Hawkins.

Tom Dorsey, after serving as one of Ma Rainey's first accompanists, made blues records on his own in the late '20s, as "Georgia Tom."

Furry Lewis.

Above: cover of a mid-'20s Victor "Race Records" catalogue and, to the right, some singers of the kind to be found therein. Many were, or at least began as, obscure backwoods performers, recorded "in the field" (Tennessee, Mississippi) for issuance almost entirely for home-area consumption —but more than a few of them became big sellers. *Below:* Recent "rediscovery" has returned some to the studios, including "Sleepy John" Estes (at *right* in left-hand photo) and Mississippi John Hurt.

Scrapper Blackwell and Leroy Carr.

Ida May Mack.

Mississippi
John Hurt

On the facing page: A most striking on-stage picture of Bessie Smith, whose title of Empress of the Blues was no exaggeration at all. During most of the '20s her incredibly rich contralto made her a Negro vaudeville-circuit headliner and a major record star, but heavy drinking curtailed her career after 1930 and in 1937 she died, after having been refused admission to a white Southern hospital following an automobile accident.

Lizzie Miles in 1929. Her career stretches back to earliest recording days: hers were among the first blues discs released in England, in 1923.

A rare photo of Sara Martin, a powerful singer and dynamic stage personality. With her in this 1923 picture is pianist-songwriter-bandleader-music publisher Clarence Williams.

A fine guitarist by any standard, jazz or blues, Lonnie Johnson recorded with the Duke Ellington Band and made some memorable duets with Eddie Lang in the '20s, remained a best-selling "race" artist through the '30s, and has had periodic brief resurgences from time to time ever since (*above*).

Bertha "Chippie" Hill was a big name among 1920s Chicago blues singers, then returned after a twenty-year layoff to give New York a taste of the real old thing in the late '40s.

Mance Lipscomb, Texas songster

Big Joe Williams, Mississippi singer and 9-string guitarist

Henry Brown, St. Louis blues singer and pianist

Eddie "Son" House, of Mississippi, had recorded for Paramount. Williams had made some of that label's very last sides, in 1931, as "King Solomon Hill"; Brown had recorded in the '20s; all—and others like them—retained the spirit and style of the old country blues, or something very close to it. They were still active, live, and on new recordings, for a limited but enthusiastic audience, into the mid-'60s.

At the left, an early (circa 1940) example of that curious phenomenon—the taking-over of country blues singers by folk-song enthusiasts (or is it vice versa?). At New York's Café Society Downtown, white-haired Hudie Ledbetter ("Leadbelly"), who had been brought North by folklorist John Lomax and rather surprisingly became a night club attraction of the '40s. His singing stayed rough-hewn, but audiences did sometimes give the impression of being at a seminar. The other guitarist is Josh White, who once led Blind Lemon and eventually went all the way over to a mannered "folksinger" style.

Sonny Terry

Blind Sonny Terry was also a blues man (notably a harmonica player) who became designated as a folk artist, and much the same path has been followed by pianist-singer "Memphis Slim" and bassist Willie Dixon *(right)*, who met with much success in post-war Europe. But the classic case was Big Bill Broonzy *(left)*, whose career as a very best-selling "race" record artist of the 1930s was overlooked by or unknown to his folk audience of the '40s and '50s, who considered him to be a recent ex-sharecropper.

The late 1940s and early '50s witnessed the rise of performers some purists would like to relegate to the "rhythm and blues" category, but critic Sam Charters calls one of them, Sam "Lightnin'" Hopkins *(left)*, "perhaps the last of the great blues singers." Many also assert the authenticity (at times) and impact (almost always) of men like John Lee Hooker *(right)* and Muddy Waters, shown looking respectively animated and cynical in the photo just above.

Both Aaron "T-Bone" Walker *(middle, left)* and big Joe Turner *(left)*, one-time Kansas City sidekick of pianist Pete Johnson, moved into the "r & b" field in the '40s and '50s with some success and no real alteration of blues style—but Jimmy Rushing *(right)* also out of K.C. and with Count Basie from 1935 to '50, has stayed with the jazz end of the blues spectrum throughout his career.

Ray Charles

Dinah Washington

In one very real sense, of course, the traditional blues are dead and have been for a long time. The old music is a superb music and the work of preserving it (whether by a Pete Welding tastefully recording a Mance Lipscomb, or by the naïve folk-izing of a Bill Broonzy) is of great value. But the blues set out to be a direct expression of a particular people and time and particular places—in that sense, of course, it *was* a folk music. That context is gone now, and so the old blues can no longer serve *that* purpose.

The sophisticated singer is not necessarily or automatically successor to the country blues man or the "classic" blues queen of the '20s. But when, once in a long while, an artist comes along with the capacity to do for his context very much what the earlier performers did for theirs, that truth shines through clearly and reassuringly. Ray Charles is a pop singer, a rhythm and blues singer, a huge commercial success; the same was true often enough of Dinah Washington before her death in 1963. But that does nothing at all to diminish or tarnish the plain fact that both are also great blues singers of their day. It is a fact that strongly suggests that the blues will really never die.

7

Pitchin' Boogie

IN THE deep South, and then in Chicago (and in such intermediate stops as Kansas City and St. Louis), they were playing that barrelhouse piano music long before "eight to the bar" became stylish. Like the blues—to which it bears a very close relationship—this is a jazz form with a cloudy early history, a music first played out in the back country by men whose life stories we'll never know.

Indications are that the piano style that has become known as "boogie woogie" had its beginnings at roughly the same time as the earliest New Orleans jazz, although quite separately. According to one account, it was originally called "fast Western," a reference to the fact that it first flourished in Texas and in towns on the western side of the Mississippi. There, among workers in the turpentine camps and railroad construction camps, this rough-hewn and fast-moving way of pounding the piano developed. Later it was carried afield by wanderers who played in saloons and backrooms and who eventually brought their music toward the cities of the Midwest, following much the same sort of path as the homeless, guitar-strumming folk-blues singers.

By the early 1920s, boogie woogie was a firmly established part of the Chicago scene, already shaped into a precise form: short, percussive phrases improvised by the right hand against the steady, rolling bass set up by the left. The term boogie woogie, of indeterminate origin, actually did not come into general use until the very end of the '20s, after it was used as the title of a recording by a pianist called Pine Top Smith. Until then, it was merely considered an aspect of barrelhouse piano—an apt term that specifically refers to the sort of saloon where liquor was served straight out of kegs. It is also quite clearly a variation of the blues, although it evolved its own special playing techniques, and there are distinct similarities between this style and that of early blues guitarists.

But nomenclature and derivations were the last things in the world to concern the men who played through the night on battered and often off-key uprights in small bars and at the incredible, free-wheeling "rent parties" in places like Chicago's South Side during the '20s and the leaner '30s. There the music was the property of formidable pianists with picturesque names—Pine Top, Cripple Clarence, Speckled Red, Cow Cow—and of quiet "Papa" Jimmy Yancey, and the slightly younger men like Meade Lux Lewis, Albert Ammons, and Pete Johnson from Kansas City. Chicago was the hub, at least partly because it was the center of recording activities, and many pianists came there briefly, from St. Louis, from Detroit—and then went home again, so that they (and for that matter, more than a few Chicago men, too) are today merely faceless names on the labels of rare old records.

Theirs was (as jazz critic William Russell has put it) "music constructed out of the piano keyboard rather than a harmony book." They were musically unlearned men, but it is precisely this "limitation" which seems the source of the music's power, of its ability to disregard the rules successfully, and of what can be called its integrity. When Ammons and Lewis and Johnson were decked out in tuxedos and, rather incongruously, became stars of concerts and swank night clubs, they still continued to play the authentic stuff, which was surely some indication of the validity of this rugged old form of manhandling the piano.

"Papa" Jimmy Yancey, in 1939.

81

The mid-1930s were both too early and too late for boogie woogie: the recording and rent-party days of the '20s were gone, and the boogie woogie fad was yet to come. Few were so soundly schooled in music or as adaptable as Albert Ammons, who weathered those years by leading bands, such as this 1936 group, shown at the Club De Lisa in Chicago.

On the far left is Jimmy Yancey, in front of his home, in 1939; at the far right, Cripple Clarence Lofton, who has always played his savage piano style in obscure South Side dives. Between them, two views of Cow Cow Davenport, one of the earliest of boogie woogie players, in the '30s and (at the microphone) in the late 1940's.

In the two snapshots at the top of the page, Meade Lux Lewis *(rear)* and Albert Ammons, in 1938, provide informal entertainment at a friend's home. But before the following year was over, their boom was on: Meade, in full dress attire, is now at a night-club grand piano.

Pete Johnson (*left*) is shown with Albert Ammons in the top photo and again, by himself. These two and Meade Lewis, working and recording separately and together (sometimes all three on the same bill), were the first to benefit, but even they must have found it odd when boogie woogie became, in the very early '40s, a national craze of frightening proportions, taken up by just about every life-of-the-party amateur in the land and by many a commercial dance band. Even Jimmy Yancey made records, but quiet Papa Jimmy felt he had retired years ago, and the studies of him at the piano in his home, on the facing page, are most typical. The fad subsided, as such things do. Yancey, Ammons and virtually every one of the authentic stylists are dead, many of the older players not even leaving a traceable photograph. Almost all that remains is the memory of this strange piano form, rugged, exciting, and a little unbelievable, crazily happy and melancholy at almost the same time.

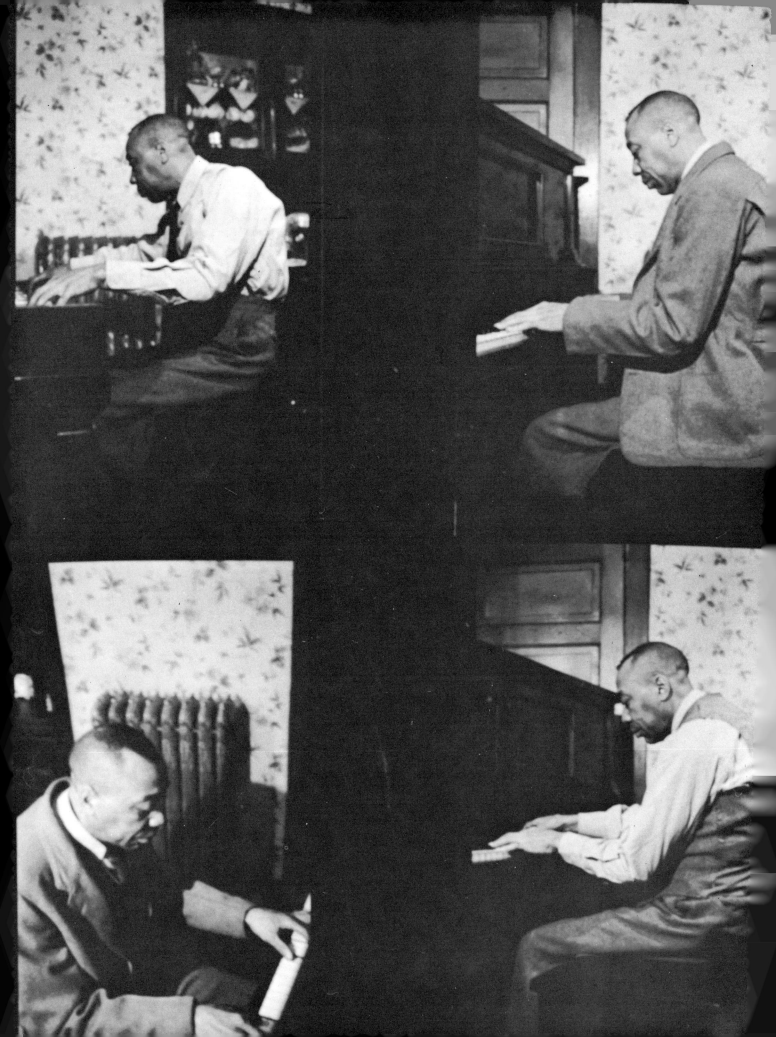

BACK TO THE
OLD HOME TOWN

8

Friars Point Shuffle

THOSE COCKY youngsters, like the Austin High Gang, and Muggsy Spanier, Eddie Condon, George Wettling, listening so hard to the music over on Chicago's South Side and to the New Orleans Rhythm Kings at Friars Inn—they were the starting point for a whole new phase of jazz.

The boys from Austin High School—Jimmy McPartland, Bud Freeman and the short-lived Frank Teschemacher were among them—can be considered as the first. At least they had something of a head start, because they all happened to be sitting around together when they heard the music for the first time. It had the same sort of effect on all of them, so they all bought instruments and taught themselves, and without even giving it much thought they found they were a band. According to the story, and it seems a well-authenticated one, someone put a New Orleans Rhythm Kings record on the victrola at the soda fountain where these boys hung out. That was in 1922, and from that moment on the music had them in its clutches. They learned from records and from hanging around the doorway of the Friars Inn (they were too young to be allowed inside). After that, they played jazz around town, first for fun and then at dances and at clubs, and almost unexpectedly they found they were full-fledged professionals, and that this was their life's work.

It wasn't by any means the Austin High gang all by itself, of course. They mixed in with a lot of others who were learning about jazz in somewhat the same way. But these others (Spanier, Mezzrow, Joe Sullivan) were more apt to be found on the South Side, were soaking up the music of Louis and Oliver, Dodds and Noone. They were under-age, too, but sometimes had better luck (Muggsy knew the owner of the Dreamland, and was allowed to slip into a corner of the balcony). Soon enough their music and the NORK-inspired jazz of Austin High merged, as they worked together in dance halls and speakeasies all over town. Before too long it became apparent that what they had was something different from any New Orleans brand of music. Out of that source material, as filtered through to them by way of the Chicago Negroes and NORK, they had founded a whole new school of jazz. When people got around to calling it by a formal name and dissecting it in books and record-album notes, it became known (obviously enough) as "Chicago style," or—to distinguish it from the South Side music—"white Chicago." It was fairly close to Negro jazz in its on-the-beat rhythms and sharply-defined notes, but it had a new swing and aggressiveness all its own.

The newness of their music does much to support the contention that jazz is inevitably greatly shaped by its immediate environment. Just as New Orleans style is clearly the product of street parades and of Storyville, so does this Chicago jazz belong, unmistakably, to the Windy City and the Roaring Twenties. It was the era of bathtub gin and tough speakeasies and Al Capone. Chicago was a hardboiled night-life town, its mood dominated by tough-guy hoods (almost every Chicago musician has at least one story to tell of playing in a mob-owned joint while it was shot up by a rival gang, or the like). The boys themselves lived high and hard during those few years' playing time in which they first evolved their own jazz style. And the music came out sounding like all that: hardboiled, sometimes harsh and driven, always with a tremendous vitality.

Mezz Mezzrow (*left*), Frank Teschemacher (*right*) before 1930.

In this battered old photograph of the band that played at the White City dance hall in 1926 are all of the Austin High Gang: Frank Teschemacher (wearing glasses) and Bud Freeman, saxophones; Jimmy McPartland, trumpet, and his brother Dick on banjo; Dave Tough, drums; Floyd O'Brien, trombone; Jim Lanigan, bass; Dave North, piano. They called themselves Husk O'Hare's Wolverines, taking the name of Bix Beiderbecke's first band, and Bix and Louis Armstrong, too, came to listen.

This is Husk O'Hare's Super-Orchestra of Chicago, of unknown personnel and undoubtedly of precious little jazz content. O'Hare was no musician, he was a promoter. But he would seem to rate inclusion here if only for having promoted both a radio job and the White City engagement for the young Chicagoans, for this was the real starting point of their careers.

Picture of two young Chicagoans earning a living the hard way: Joe Sullivan, at the piano, and saxophonist Bud Jacobson (*fourth from left*) in a dance band led by Frank Boyle, Jr., in the late '20s.

At the left, in an amusement-park photographer's studio (the phony observation car is the same as the one on page 86): Jess Stacy (*left*), Teschemacher (*right*), George Wettling and bride, in 1929. The three curly-haired young men in the middle photo are (*left to right*): Benny Goodman, Jimmy McPartland, Bud Freeman. At the right is a snapshot of Teschemacher and his dogs, taken by Wettling.

Chicagoan Red McKenzie, who developed "blue-blowing" (tissue-paper and comb, played in trumpet-imitation style) into something of an art, was the leader of the highly popular Mound City Blue Blowers in 1924. Others were Dick Slevin (left) on kazoo; Jack Bland, banjo; and guitarist Eddie Lang.

"Photographs made in fifteen minutes" says the inscription on the back of these 1927 pictures. It would seem that despite the worried looks on Jess Stacy (left), George Wettling and Frank Teschemacher (standing), in the left-hand photo, the promise was kept. At least Jess and George looked happier when they posed again, with Muggsy Spanier.

The 1940 Collector's Item Cats recording session marked a return to jazz circles for cornetist Wild Bill Davison. Up to this point Davison had been primarily known as the driver of the car on the night Teschemacher was killed in a crash. He went on to play a major part in the New York Dixieland movement. Boyce Brown, on alto saxophone, was a near-legendary figure who entered a monastery in the mid-'50s, died in 1959.

These are pictures of the 1940s: bassist Jim Lanigan, an Austin High boy who remained a part of the Chicago scene; and Volly De Faut, who recorded with Muggsy Spanier and once with Jelly Roll Morton in the '20s, but did not become active again in the Chicago picture until the post-war period.

Pee Wee Russell.

Rod Cless.

Muggsy Spanier.

Bud Freeman.

Joe Sullivan.

Eddie Condon.

There are some revealing comments to be made about the last few pages of this chapter. Between pages 90 and 91 there is a sudden leap of more than a decade. And the pictures of leading Chicagoans shown on this and the facing page, while not showing them as they are today, are not photographs from the '20s. These two factors fit together to make a point, which is that during the '30s there were just about no original Chicagoans left in town. By the close of the '20s, many of them had gone on to New York permanently, while others were somewhat like commuters. The center of the jazz world was quickly shifting eastward: the depression of the '30s wrecked the midwestern independent record companies, and the end of Prohibition put a crimp in Chicago's special night life. Thus the era of "Chicago style" was most brief, at least in its home town, and these last pages present a picture gallery of men who were henceforth to belong to New York jazz, primarily, and therefore to a later chapter.

9

Bixology

Bix Beiderbecke was obviously the sort of man about whom legends insist upon growing. He lived for only twenty-eight years, and his career actually spanned less than a decade (most of that time spent in bands that could not do justice to his sensitive, lyric jazz talents). Yet he was a tremendous influence on all the musicians who heard him: the Chicagoans, not much younger than he, made him their idol; and such listeners as Louis Armstrong, Red Nichols, and the men who worked alongside him in the Paul Whiteman and Jean Goldkette orchestras seem to have been uniformly awed and amazed. He remains a vivid, affectionate and larger than life-size memory to almost all who knew him—and to a great many who didn't. He remains, in short, the number-one jazz legend.

The basic facts of his life can readily be stated. He was Leon Bismarck Beiderbecke, born in Davenport, Iowa, on March 10, 1903. From a well-to-do and musically-inclined family, he studied piano a bit, soon switched to cornet, but probably never took a lesson on that instrument in his life. By the time he entered Chicago's Lake Forest Academy, in 1921, he would seem to have discovered jazz and to have been set on following it. He soon left school to become part of a young band called the Wolverines, playing at roadhouses and at college dances. He left them late in 1924 to begin a hectic half-decade ride to the top and the end: featured with the bands of Frankie Trumbauer, Goldkette, finally Whiteman, where his round, firm notes cut through the thick-syrup arrangements of that "King of Jazz." Briefly, Bix was brilliant, but he burned out fast. The high, fast living, the bad whiskey and worse gin of Pro-

hibition, were rather quickly too much for the small, slightly pop-eyed cornetist. He was sick and out of the Whiteman band during his last year and in August of 1931 he was dead, of pneumonia.

Thus, significantly, the legends did not spring up because the facts were little known or far removed. On the contrary, you could talk today with musicians who knew him well. And chances are that they'd tell the familiar larger-than-life versions of what are undoubtedly basically true stories (Bix as a heavy drinker, a practical joker, sensationally absent-minded; accounts of fabulous after-hours jam sessions). Or they might add a new story or two, and they'd surely tell them with a warmly reminiscent smile. For it's clear that such men really loved Bix, found him brother and awesome genius and irresponsible son all in one. *They* have built the legend, as much or more than any romantically-minded outsiders; they *want* to remember him as someone special and touched with myth. Taking the stories, and the way in which they are told, and adding to them the pure, beautiful, but somehow tense quality of the sound that tumbled forth from his horn, a definable pattern seems to emerge. It is a picture of a vastly complex man, rather reminiscent of an F. Scott Fitzgerald hero, driven by a great love of beauty and of music, perhaps trying to conceal the fact that he was more than a bit bewildered and frightened by the things that make up everyday life. An immense talent and a man to whom everyone's heart went out, but basically unreachable and self-doomed, almost a stereotype of a standard hero of current fiction—the artist in conflict with himself and with the world in which he had to live.

These two pages are devoted to a band that would probably be dismissed as mediocre if Bix Beiderbecke had not been its cornetist, if this had not been the group with which he was first heard. The full Wolverine Orchestra personnel, in addition to Bix, was: Al Gande, trombone; Jimmy Hartwell, clarinet; George Johnson, tenor sax; Dick Voynow, piano; Bob Gillette, banjo; Min Leibrook, tuba; Vic Moore, drums. All are present in the top photo, taken when they made their first appearance in Chicago in 1923; and at the time of their first Gennett recording date, February 18, 1924.

Recording Information of Wax No. 11854
11854A
11854B

Date Recorded 5-6-24   By E. C. A. Wickemeyer   At Richmond, Ind.

Subject Riverboat Shuffle

By Wolverine Orchestra   Accompanied by

Composed by   Music by Carmichael

Words by Carmichael   Published by Hoaglund Carmichael
Kappa Sigma House, Bloomington, Indiana
Copyright   19   Royalties   1924

Exterior of the warehouse where Gennett records were made, Richmond, Indiana. When freight trains passed on these tracks, all recording activity paused.

Gande dropped out after the first records, and they remained without a trombone for such slightly later recordings as *Riverboat Shuffle*, and for their engagement at the Cinderella Ballroom in New York, late in 1924, which is when this bottom photo was taken. Shortly thereafter, Bix left the band (Jimmy McPartland was his replacement) for bigger orchestras and bigger things.

With some of the Chicagoans who admired him. In this battered and torn snapshot are *(seated, left to right):* Pee Wee Russell, Mezz Mezzrow, Bix, Eddie Condon.

Bix's early and close friend, Hoagy Carmichael, the very same Hoaglund (see top of page 97) who wrote, among many other songs, *Riverboat Shuffle.*

Jean Goldkette's orchestra at their ease, in about 1927. Bix sprawls on the ground, wearing a sleeveless sweater. At his right is Tommy Dorsey, with Don Murray standing behind him.

A later photo of Frank Trumbauer, close friend and co-worker on many a job and recording date.

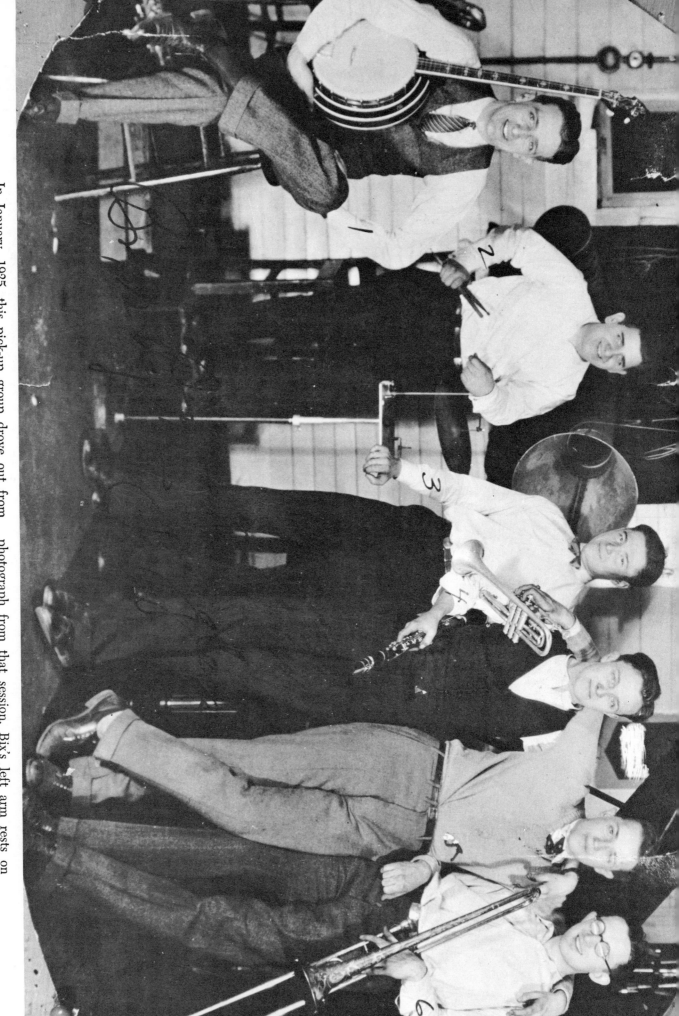

In January, 1925, this pick-up group drove out from Chicago to the Gennett studios in Richmond, Indiana, to make the first recordings issued under Beiderbecke's name ("Bix and his Rhythm Jugglers"). In this rare photograph from that session, Bix's left arm rests on Tommy Dorsey's shoulder, his right on Don Murray. The others (*left to right*) are Howdy Quicksell, drummer Tommy Gargano, pianist Paul Mertz.

Photographs of the Paul Whiteman band including Bix are exceedingly rare. Beiderbecke, with a new moustache and a wide smile, is third from the right in the rear row. Frank Trumbauer is half-hidden behind the tuba; Don Murray (*second from right, second row*) and Izzy Friedman, who is seated at Whiteman's left, were with him in this 1928 band. The Victor recording sheet indicates one of Bix's very first records with Whiteman: with Carmichael and the Dorseys on hand, and comparatively stripped-down instrumentation, it may have seemed to promise more musical satisfaction than this huge, semi-symphonic orchestra was actually able to give him.

3304

Records by: Whitemans Orchestra

98 CONTINUE

Marking	Letter	Pitch	Serial Number	Matrix Number	SELECTION. COMPOSER, PUBLISHER, ETC.	Wax	Rec.	F. Cur.	Amp. Set	Level	F. I.
					Chicago Lab. Nov.18th,1927. Whiteman Dir. Shields Present. Instr. 2Violin,Viola,2Sax,Clarinet,Cornet,2Trombone,Bass, Guitar,Vibraphone,Bass Clarinet, (Piano By)("Hoagy" Carmichael.)						
M	CVE	100	40901	1	Washboard Blues	55-388	182	.9	3-3	40	0
P	CVE	100	40901	2	Comp. Carmichael & Callahan	55-375	"	"	3-3	0	0
D	CVE	100	40901	3	Pub. & Copyr, J.Mills.	55-388	"	"	4-4	2	16
HC	CVE	100	40901	4	Manuscript Verbal.	55-386	"	"	4-4	2	0
D	CVE	100	40901	5	(Vocal By "Hoagy" Carmichael)	55-387	"	"	4-4	2	0
					Names of Orchestra men:- Russel,Dieterle,Malineck,Jimmie Dorsey,Strickfadden, Biederback,T.Dorsey,Cullen,Brown,W.Hall,Mac Donald, C.Hazlet. Time:- 9:00 To 12:15 A.M. FE. GA. *Orchestration Changed in last 2 records.*						

This solemn staring-eyed photograph is from the White-man period. Then comes the stark recital of the final facts: the official death certificate notes the necessary details, including "lobar pneumonia . . . duration . . . 3 days."

10

Stomp Off, Let's Go

FLETCHER HENDERSON, and then Bill McKinney and others, had this brand-new idea of using strict written arrangements—and still keeping it mostly jazz. Before they were through, they had achieved a major revolution in jazz, less by seeking change than by, of necessity, adapting most successfully to altering circumstances. Henderson, certainly the key figure of this period, was an extremely talented arranger with more than a fair share of technical skill and fresh ideas, and an adept leader of men as well. But he did not create this music, full-grown, out of some sudden inspiration. He came to it gradually, but surely, and it seems a safe guess that his principal ambition was to build and maintain a very good dance band.

It is all too easy to forget that jazz has usually been a music to dance to. Buddy Bolden played for dancers. What he played, however, would hardly have satisfied the crowd that Henderson faced from the bandstand at Broadway's Roseland Ballroom. So, while there may be many other ways of explaining the differences between early traditional jazz and this Negro big-band music of the middle and late 1920s and thereafter, the latter is, above all, the kind of music that develops when you play at big dance halls and at night clubs with fairly fancy floor shows, when you provide the size and the sound that such circumstances demand.

Instrumentation can provide a valuable clue to the nature of the differences. To continue with Henderson as the prime example: he opened at the Club Alabam in 1922 with a ten-man group, which isn't much more than the eight with whom King Oliver was playing in a strictly traditional vein in Chicago at the same time. But those two added men were both saxophone players; the total of three, instead of a single clarinetist, made a "section." That of course is one of the key words, one of the fundamentals of big-band music. Soon enough there were also at least three trumpets and two trombones. Added to the four rhythm instruments, this mean a dozen or more men working in unison.

That unison necessitated the use of steadily more complex arrangements, and increasingly precise teamwork. To achieve this, and to do so without losing the drive and spirit that is jazz, called for a difficult combination: not only talented scoring, but also musicians capable of both handling the section parts and cutting loose effectively in those spots left open for solo work. Although no other band of the period had so consistently star-studded a lineup as Henderson's, the general level was actually amazingly high (the faces of quite a few jazzmen recognized as of the top rank are to be seen on the following pages).

Basically, this style was a New York phenomenon, nurtured in the night spots of Harlem. Even an apparent exception like McKinney's Cotton Pickers, whose home base was Detroit, used many musicians from the New York scene and, most importantly, had as its musical director a Henderson alumnus, Don Redman. It's true that Negro big-band jazz can also be considered a product of its time, rather than of a specific place: there were such groups in Chicago and in Kansas City. But Chicago bandleaders such as, say, Earl Hines or Tiny Parham were part of the overall jazz pattern of that town; and Kansas City, as shall be seen, was something of a special case. In New York, the music of Henderson, his contemporaries and those who followed in his footsteps was, in itself, just about the sum-total of the jazz band tradition.

Fletcher Henderson; a later photograph.　　103

Fletcher Henderson's 1922 band, as it opened at the Club Alabam. Time has not treated this photo kindly, deleting trombonist Charlie "Big" Green, who was at the left. The original rhythm section of Bob Escudero, tuba; Henderson; Charlie Dixon, banjo; and Kaiser Marshall, drums; as well as saxophone star Don Redman (*right*), were to remain fixtures for the next few years. Coleman Hawkins (*second from right*) remained for more than a decade. Howard Scott (*left*) and Elmer Chambers are on trumpet; and there was a third sax man, identity unremembered.

By 1927, Fletcher Henderson's Orchestra was larger, more star-studded. The leader stands at the left. Others standing are (left to right): trombonists Jimmy Harrison, Benny Morton; June Cole, tuba; drummer Marshall. Seated (left to right): banjoist Dixon; a sax section of Don Pasquall, Buster Bailey, and Hawkins; a trumpet section of Tommy Ladnier, Joe Smith, Russell Smith. The lower right-hand snapshot shows Hawkins, the master who influenced an entire generation of tenor sax men, with bespectacled Claude Jones, trombonist in the 1930 band. The left-hand photo is of Jimmy Harrison, one of the trombone greats of this era.

Still another great Henderson band, full of big-name talent, on the Atlantic City, N. J., boardwalk in 1931. Standing (*left to right*): John Kirby, bass; Hawkins once more; Russell Procope, sax; trumpeters Rex Stewart and Bobby Stark; Clarence Holiday, guitar. Seated (*left to right*): Edgar Sampson, sax; Sandy Williams and J. C. Higginbotham, trombones; Henderson; Russell Smith, trumpet; drummer Walter Johnson.

William McKinney.

McKinney's Cotton Pickers became one of the most impressive and smooth bands of the late '20s largely through the efforts of Don Redman *(sixth from left in upper photo)* as musical director. The group around the ornamental fountain at Jean Goldkette's Greystone Ballroom in Detroit (their most frequent home base) includes *(seated on the right)* the trumpet section of *(left to right)* Joe Smith, John Nesbitt, Langston Curl. Tenor sax George Thomas is seated at the far left; standing at the left are *(left to right)* pianist Todd Rhodes, banjo player Dave Wilborn, drummer Cuba Austin. In the lower picture is much the same group, plus trombonist Claude Jones *(standing, fourth from left)*. Bill McKinney, one-time drummer, confined himself to serving as business manager for his band.

A rare and incompletely identified photograph that is, at the very least, unusual. Probably taken in Atlantic City in the late '20s, it definitely includes Bessie Smith *(seated on floor, center)*, and Frankie "Half Pint" Jaxon, who is seated on top of the piano. The musicians are most probably from Charlie Johnson's Paradise Ten, a fixture at Small's Paradise and one of the very best of the early Harlem bands. Jimmy Harrison is probably the trombonist at the right; Edgar Sampson, who played violin less frequently than saxophone, stands under the "Dance" sign, and Charlie Johnson is at the piano.

Two creators of the Johnson band's noted "growling" brass sound: Charlie Irvis (after whom Duke Ellington's "Tricky Sam" Nanton patterned his muted trombone style); and Leonard Davis *(right)*.

Rex Stewart was an increasingly important figure on the Harlem jazz scene even before he was featured with Henderson, and then with Duke Ellington, in the 1930s. With him in the six-piece Society Orchestra of one Bobbie Brown *(bottom photo)* early in the '20s is saxophonist Happy Caldwell *(second from right)*; Rex is on the left. By 1924, both had moved on to pianist Willie Gant's band, at Small's Paradise *(top photo)*. Stewart bulks large in the foreground, with Happy at his right. Another fine trumpet man, Ward Pinkett, stands behind Gant *(second from left)*. In the center picture, of the Nest Club Orchestra of banjoist Elmer Snowden *(seated, left)*, Stewart stands at the right, with clarinetist Prince Robinson seated near him.

The Missourians came out of the Midwest, heavily influenced by the Bennie Moten band of Kansas City and carved out a name for themselves. In about 1930, they became the nucleus of the Cab Calloway band. This photo was taken at the Savoy Ballroom in 1926. Key members included tenor sax Andy Brown *(left)*; De Priest Wheeler, on trombone; R. Q. Dickerson, trumpet *(third from right)*; drummer Leroy Maxey.

Also out of the Midwest (Ohio) came Cecil Scott. On various road trips, his band added and thus introduced to New York trombonist Dicky Wells *(front row, left)* and trumpet star Frankie Newton *(front row, second from left)*. When they played the Savoy, in about 1928, the group had Bill Coleman as their other trumpet, Don Frye on piano, John Williams and Harold McFerran *(right)* on saxes.

Among the many Harlem homes for medium and large-sized bands was the Bamboo Inn, later known as the Dunbar Palace. In the upper photo, taken in 1928, the first name was in use; pianist Joe Steele's band is on the stand, with young trombonist Jimmy Archey *(right)*. The following year, under the new name, and apparently redecorated, they had the band shown in the lower picture. Led by Fletcher Henderson's brother Horace *(seated)*, also a pianist, this group included drummer Manzie Johnson *(second from left)*; Sandy Williams on trombone *(fifth from right)*; John Williams, sax.

111

American jazz was exported to Europe quite early. This band led by pianist Sam Wooding, which recorded in Berlin in 1924, is shown onstage in Copenhagen in the bottom photo. Grouped above are the orchestra's several notable members, including New Orleans trumpeter Tommy Ladnier *(seated, left, in light suit)* and *(standing)* Herb Flemming, trombone *(left)*; Gene Sedric *(third from left)* and Garvin Bushell *(third from right)*, saxophonists.

Noble Sissle's Orchestra was also widely traveled. This 1929 photograph was taken in Paris. Clarinetist Buster Bailey is at the far right.

A little-known group with some intriguing personnel: Jap Allen's Orchestra. Tenor sax star Ben Webster is seated at the left; next to him is pianist Clyde Hart. Both continued on into modern jazz, with Hart appearing on some 1945 Dizzy Gillespie recordings. Also, trumpeter Joe Keyes (*far left*) and Webster had been with Bennie Moten's Kansas City band, and Keyes is on Count Basie's first recordings. This, plus long Oklahoma and Kansas City bookings noted on the back of the photo, seem to place this as a Midwest-formed band of the early 1930s.

Little Chick Webb *(insert; and center, rear)* came up from Baltimore in the mid-20s, and finally put together a band that was a fixture at the Savoy Ballroom between 1931 and 1935. This picture, from fairly early in that period, includes Taft Jordan *(left)* and Louis Bacon *(second from left)* on trumpets; trombonist Sandy Williams; and also sax man Edgar Sampson *(seated third from right)*, an increasingly active arranger.

Claude Hopkins' band of the mid-30s affords a rare glimpse of a neglected trumpet man of great talent: Jabbo Smith, leaning over Hopkins' piano *(front row, fourth from left)*. Trombonist Vic Dickenson is at his left, trumpeter Shirley Clay at his right. (The photo is autographed by Jabbo to his mother.)

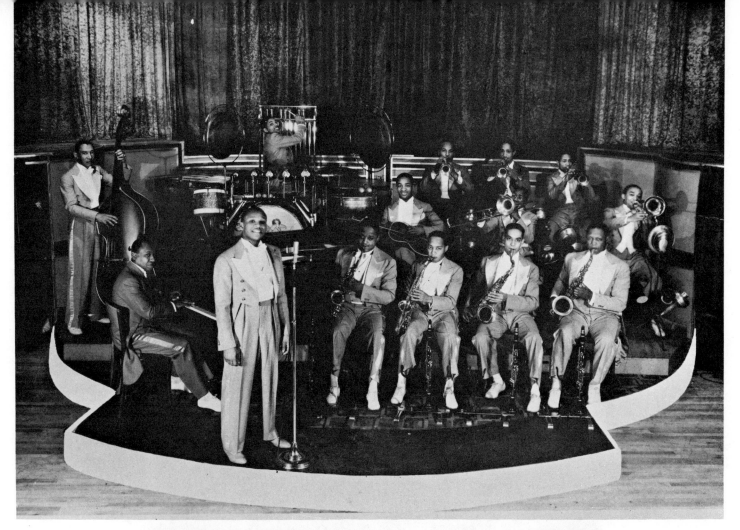

In the top photograph is the 1935 band of pianist Luis Russell. He had played in Storyville (page 10) and with a King Oliver group in Chicago (page 32), and from the late '20s on was a most successful bandleader. Trombonist Jimmy Archey (*second row, center*) and Pops Foster, bass, are among the personnel here. Meanwhile, Oliver had been on a downhill road; coming to New York in about 1928, he had been dogged by bad luck and then bad health. He was on the road with this unidentified group in the mid-30s (significantly, the inset photo of Oliver is from an earlier day). Stranded in Savannah, Georgia, he died in 1938. By then, his day was long over; the music of Fletcher Henderson and the men who followed his pattern had brought jazz to the era of Swing.

Sincerely
Lawrence Welk

11

Turn On the Heat

You COULDN'T always think of the Paul Whiteman or Jean Goldkette orchestras as jazz bands, but there were always some pretty fair hot musicians on hand. And both within the frameworks of such bands and on their excursions outside them, those individuals managed to produce a quantity of good, tough, honest jazz—although it sometimes took quite some doing.

The background and the musical atmosphere of these large bands (and they were indeed large: Whiteman's personnel, including violins and vocalists, often got up into the thirties) was basically different from that of the big Negro bands noted in the preceding chapter. For one thing, these orchestras were catering to a much wider and more generalized audience: big ballrooms, hotel dance floors, the major vaudeville and movie theaters were their usual settings. Thus, no matter what their intentions, jazz—in any true sense of the word—certainly could not be a primary consideration. At best it can be said that they made much use of jazz and semi-jazz conceptions in their dance music. Whiteman's billing as "King of Jazz" should not be taken too seriously in a musical sense; no more so than the overall designation of all the goings-on of the Roaring Twenties as "The Jazz Age." But he was a friend and steady employer of bona fide jazz musicians, and the same was true of Jean Goldkette: Beiderbecke, Joe Venuti and Eddie Lang, the young Dorsey brothers, Frank Trumbauer and others spent more than a little time with both these groups.

This was very much a period of change and fusion of styles for many white jazzmen, of moving from one band to another and, particularly, of alternating big-band work with prolific small-group recording activity. Red Nichols and Miff Mole were the standout figures in this phase. As a team on innumerable records they seem to epitomize small-band jazz of this sort; and a sampling of Nichols' activities during the '20s can indicate how hectic and varied it all was: playing with Whiteman, in musical-comedy pit bands, and on records with (at one time or another) just about every white musician in town.

Throughout the '20s, New York remained the place to be, the place where the best, if not precisely all, of the big-band jobs were. Late in the decade, a good many of the Chicago crowd were among those pouring into town, and more than a few came by way of another band that pretty much fitted the semi-jazz pattern: Ben Pollack's. The difference here was that this was a group organized by a jazzman (Pollack had been the New Orleans Rhythm Kings drummer). His intention was to qualify for those big-money dance band jobs, yet still allow room for solo work by his many talented employees: Benny Goodman, Jimmy McPartland and later Jack Teagarden among them. He succeeded rather well, and the men who came into town with him helped add another facet to the already hybrid small-band recording and jam session style. Conditioned by just about all the currents then flowing through white jazz, this style included as well the continuing influence of the Original Dixieland Jazz Band, and bore the marks of the big-band techniques to which most of the players were exposed. All this and more made up a mixture that amounts to "New York Dixieland." The reverse side of the coin from the big orchestras, it provided these musicians with an opportunity to "turn on the heat" with considerable regularity and freedom.

Paul Whiteman's Orchestra, 1928.

Throughout the 1920s and on into the '30s, Paul Whiteman employed a good many jazz musicians, who usually found "Pops" to be a friend and the well-paying confines of his huge orchestra quite bearable for a while, at least. Jack Teagarden *(top row, left)*, in this 1933 band, was a prominently featured soloist. And when Whiteman made Mildred Bailey the first girl ever to sing regularly with a band, in 1931, he launched a notable jazz career.

Mildred Bailey.

Ted Lewis was strictly a master of corn, but in the late '20s some jazzmen found steady work with him to be a welcome change from the usual scuffle. In the front row sits an already-stocky George Brunies *(second from left)*, with Muggsy Spanier at his left.

Eddie Lang (*left*) and Joe Venuti—two of the outstanding figures of this period, both as members of the Goldkette and Whiteman orchestras and as most important parts of the small-unit recording scene in New York. They made up perhaps the most famous two-man team in jazz (with the possible exception of Red Nichols and Miff Mole, of course). Venuti was one of the few really effective jazz violinists, and Lang was in large part responsible for the general switch from banjo to guitar at the turn of the '30s.

The Coon-Sanders Orchestra, one of the most popular in its day, which was *circa* 1930. Not really a jazz group in any strict sense, they represent what the public often tended to accept as jazz.

There were college jazz bands back in those days, too. This 1923 photograph appeared in the Harvard Lampoon as an advertisement for this Original Hot Five, which included Jim Moynahan on clarinet and trombonist Brad Gowans, later to be an important member of the Eddie Condon Dixieland crowd in New York.

Bailey's Lucky Seven recording for Gennett in New York in 1923. Since this band-name was used to cover a shifting personnel that often involved members of Phil Napoleon's Original Memphis Five, and since almost everyone here is turned away from the camera, this picture has become the source of a long-standing guessing game. The trombonist is almost surely Miff Mole. Eddie Lang may possibly be on banjo (which he played prior to 1924). The clarinetist looks like Benny Goodman, but can't be (he was a 14-year-old in Chicago at the time).

Adrian Rollini was an ever-present factor on recordings of the Red Nichols variety, and his bass saxophone gave a distinctive sound to The California Ramblers, a largely-jazz big band that included Red Nichols and the Dorsey brothers.

A band of indeterminate jazz value, but featuring a rare profile shot of a pianist named Jimmy Durante. Clarinetist Achille Baquet had played in early Jack Laine bands in New Orleans.

Joe Tarto (left) and Leo McConville were frequent associates of Red Nichols, and the trumpeter went on to play with the Dorsey Brothers band. Tarto's freak tuba—eight feet high—was designed for his appearance in the pit band Nichols led for the musical comedy, "Rain or Shine," in 1928.

121

Miff Mole seemed to be everywhere on the New York jazz scene during the '20s, usually in the outstanding small groups of the day. But the photograph at the top of the page finds him *(second from right)* in the early dance band of Roger Wolfe Kahn, which also included Joe Venuti *(third from left)*. More customary settings for Miff were Red Nichols' Five Pennies *(center photo)*, whose six-man lineup here included *(left to right)*: Red, Jimmy Dorsey, Arthur Schutt, Vic Berton, Mole, Eddie Lang; and the Original Memphis Five, which in the picture at the right includes Phil Napoleon on trumpet, pianist Frank Signorelli, Mole and clarinetist Jimmy Lytell.

The Jean Goldkette Orchestra provided many top performers with at least moderate opportunity to play jazz, until it broke up late in 1927, largely as a result of an over-heavy load of payroll and temperament. Here they pose outside the bus that carried them on a tour of New England. Bix Beiderbecke is fourth from the right, and Steve Brown, one-time New Orleans Rhythm Kings bassist, is second from the right.

These two can sum up this hectic era of big bands, small units, Prohibition and the Roaring Twenties. Loring "Red" Nichols, one of the giants of the period, is still playing Dixieland horn in California. Guitarist Eddie Lang, one of the finest musicians of his day, died in the early '30s.

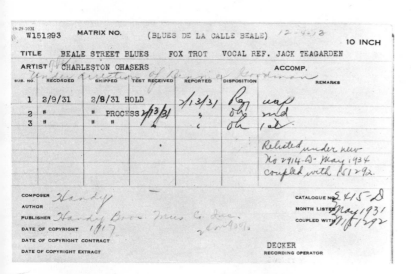

The Charleston Chasers name covered a variety of recording lineups, including Nichols, Napoleon, the Dorseys, and such newcomers as Jack Teagarden and Benny Goodman. Benny had come to New York from Chicago with the band led by Ben Pollack; in the picture on the facing page, the year is 1928 and he is a youthful 19. Others in this photo are Jack Teagarden, with Jimmy McPartland at his left, and drummer Ray Bauduc. Besides bringing this new talent onto the scene, this band provides more than a hint of the Swing Era to come: by its use of almost entirely jazz personnel in a jazz-and-dance orchestra, and by giving Goodman his start. In 1935, Pollack's band was taken over by Bob Crosby and became one of the earliest Swing groups.

12

Harlem Strut

THERE WERE more good piano men than you could count, but it wasn't really a party without Fats Waller or James P. Johnson on hand to give the keyboard a thorough workout. These two were the prime movers of a leaping, stomping form of jazz that was the other part of the Harlem jazz story: pre-dating, contemporary with, and eventually outlasting the big band music. The outlasting was done largely by Waller, whose unique and infectious approach to popular song remained everyone's delight right up until his death in 1943. The pre-dating refers to such as Jimmy Johnson, who began his long career before the 1920s.

The music with which Waller began and with which Johnson and a number of other talented, dazzling piano men remained, is probably best described by turning to its basic setting during the '20s, the raucous, colorful "rent party." This rather widespread phenomenon (its Midwestern equivalent has been noted in passing in the earlier chapter on boogie woogie piano) originally was literally a device for rounding up the rent money by crowding as many friends as possible into an apartment and having them pay for an evening of food, drink and entertainment. This specific purpose may have been ignored before long, but the parties became a staple item at, seemingly, every flat that boasted a piano in working condition. Usually only one pianist was hired for such a job, but before the long, wild night was over, many more were likely to be around. The fiercely competitive, high-spirited "cutting contests" were of legendary intensity—with James P., men known by such names as The Beetle and Lippy, and maybe a precocious youngster like Tom Waller or Duke Ellington, all taking their turns at the piano until dawn.

Ragtime, which was at the height of its popularity in New York during most of the second decade of the century, had a strong influence on the style of Johnson and the other older players. Stomping variations of rags, known as "shouts," were the show-pieces most often used in competition; they were ideally suited to be heard over the normal party din. There were also liberal added dashes of both the blues and the brash sound of early Broadway show tunes (James P. wrote the songs for all-Negro musicals of the day, with *Old Fashioned Love* the most famous of a long list). This made up the essence of Harlem piano. It was this that Johnson helped bring out in his protégé, Fats Waller. And of course it was by way of Waller's particular interpretation of it that this music was to become most widely known. Fats' voice and his way of cutting a less-than-ordinary ballad apart, turning even the most banal material into an extraordinary musical experience—this was clearly his personal accomplishment, the product of his own special personality. But the foundation of his music was established here, in the world of the Harlem theaters where he was organist, at the small bars and the rent parties.

With their combination of competitiveness and tight-knit camaraderie, and their important role in the not-strictly-professional social life of the community, these Harlem pianists seem akin to the early New Orleans musicians. But most of them were musically well-educated, unlike either the New Orleans pioneers or the Chicago rent party men. Their music, though limited in form, covers a wide range of emotions, sometimes moody, more often swift and happy—the sort of variety that is usually the mark of the best of jazz.

Fats Waller at the organ.

Clarence Williams, who had played piano in New Orleans, became a most influential figure in New York in the '20s, as a music publisher and as leader of various groups on a substantial number of recordings. King Oliver was on some of these, but not as many as some people have thought. Ed Allen, shown here, sounded enough like him to fool them. Others in this group are Prince Robinson and washboard-player Floyd Casey. The business card provides an interesting comparison with those of Jelly Roll Morton (page 66).

Willie the Lion Smith, who has infinite explanations of how he came by that nickname, was among the most celebrated rent-party pianists of the '20s, and is still quite active.

Perry Bradford, like Clarence Williams, was pianist, publisher and an organizer of record dates. Two of his 1924 Jazz Hounds are June Clark on trumpet, and trombonist Jimmy Harrison, who formed a famous Harlem brass team in the early '20s. In this photo, Bradford is standing behind the piano.

Harlem was drawing young talent eastward even while Chicago was still the center of jazz. Scott's Symphonic Syncopators, shown here in a 1923 photo, began in Springfield, Ohio, and were playing in New York by 1925. Cecil Scott is the saxophonist, Lloyd Scott the drummer. On piano is Don Frye, most celebrated in later years as an intermission pianist in downtown clubs.

A very early snapshot, perhaps pre-1920, of the dean of
Harlem pianists, James P. Johnson.

James P. was a more adaptable musician than many other pianists of the Harlem rent-party school. He led bands in Harlem in the early '30s, and in the '40s became very much a part of the Dixieland-and-jam-session activities downtown. In the top photo is the band he led at the Apollo Theater and Small's Paradise in 1934-35. Ex-Henderson trumpet man Howard Scott stands directly behind Johnson. For a Westchester Country Club job several years later, James P. had Joe Thomas on trumpet, Manzie Johnson on drums.

Thomas "Fats" Waller was unquestionably unique: satirist, clown, and a fine pianist who learned the ropes from James P. Johnson and at many a rent party. Here is Waller, family, and friends.

With songwriter Spencer Williams, in Brighton, England, during a 1938 tour.

With his son, Maurice, in the late '30s.

With his wife, Anita, in Scotland, summer, 1938.

A pose that seems to express a good deal of the Waller personality. In Phoenix, Arizona, probably 1937.

Andy Razaf, lyricist for *Ain't Misbehavin'*, *Honeysuckle Rose*, and many other Waller hits. A 1949 photo.

Fats in the recording studio. In the top photograph, the place is Chicago, the date, January, 1940. Gene Sedric who played clarinet and tenor sax on the vast majority of Fats's records, is on hand in both pictures, as is bassist Cedric Wallace. Guitarist Al Casey, also a frequent member of "Fats Waller and his Rhythm," is in the lower photo. This was taken at a July, 1942, session in New York in which the Deep River Boys vocal quartet also took part.

Young Duke Ellington.

"The Beetle."

Cliff Jackson.

Willie the Lion.

Luckey Roberts.

On the facing page is a goodly sampling of Harlem piano talent (although Duke Ellington was only briefly a part of the scene in the mid-'20s before his band hit its stride). Luckey Roberts was an even earlier figure than James P. Johnson, playing in a style closer to ragtime and with a right hand capable of incredibly difficult feats. The story is that no one could play his lightning-fast *Ripples of the Nile,* so he slowed it down and it became a popular hit in 1942: *Moonlight Cocktail.* Willie the Lion Smith is much older here than on page 128, but is apparently much jauntier; he is actually the only man continuing in the "stride piano" tradition of the '20s, and like boogie woogie, this is a form that just about totally disappeared as the older men faded from the picture. There could be no better last glimpse of this music than the photograph, above, of Jimmy Johnson, cigar clamped in his teeth, scowling pensively at the piano. By November, 1955, after a long and crippling illness, Johnson was dead.

135

13

Cotton Club Stomp

DUKE ELLINGTON's music inhabits a rich, lush world of its own, and it's been that way for almost forty years now. No other band in jazz has come close to staying in existence for so long, with more than a few musicians having established truly astonishing records, in such a quick-turnover business, for length of service with one leader. No other composer has come close to creating such a string of tunes that manages to combine valid jazz feeling with whatever it is that makes a song a hit. No other big-band leader or arranger has ever mastered so thoroughly (and few have even cared to try) the difficult art of writing directly *for* each of his major sidemen—whether in building an ensemble passage or merely indicating the direction an improvised solo should take—so that the musician's strong points and the contribution, of sound or of emotion, that the band most needs from his instrument can merge and become as one. The most important clue to his success may lie in the oft-repeated comment that Ellington does not so much play piano as play a whole band, using an orchestra as a lesser musician would use a single instrument.

There has actually been an Ellington band in existence since the very early 1920s, but the first significant date is December, 1927, when the Duke and his men opened at the Cotton Club, as a last-minute replacement for a King Oliver band. They had already attracted some attention, particularly among musicians, during their first New York booking, which was at Barron's, in Harlem, and then downtown at the Kentucky Club. But the Cotton Club, where white audiences flocked to hear the "jungle music" of Harlem, was the place that could really launch a young band. And the Ellington orchestra was to prove its all-time prize package.

Edward Kennedy Ellington had first turned fully to music in 1917, when at the age of eighteen he declined an art school scholarship to become, briefly, a ragtime pianist and then leader of a small group in his home town of Washington, D.C. Coming to New York in 1923 for a job that failed to materialize, the band managed to catch on at Barron's. After that it was a slow process of building both repertoire and reputation, and gradually adding key personnel to a nucleus that already included Otto Hardwick and Sonny Greer. By 1926, having added Harry Carney and the two masters of the "growl tone," trumpeter Bubber Miley and trombonist "Tricky Sam" Nanton, they were ready for the main chance when it came along. They never needed a second try. In the years that followed, the Duke has continued to build his remarkable musical world, from the early "jungle" sound through ever-increasing sophistication and constant experimentation.

If there is any area in which the multi-talented Ellington has not always been given his just due, it is as a composer. In a sense, he has cheated himself, for he has always been a composer-in-action: the emphasis is inevitably on the performance (by his orchestra, usually in his arrangement) rather than on the material itself. But from the mood music that characterized his earliest bands (*Black and Tan Fantasy, Mood Indigo, Creole Love Call*), through the beautiful melodies that became hits (and those, equally lovely, that didn't), and the brief concertos for various solo stars, on to the more ambitious and never quite fully accepted longer pieces like *Black, Brown and Beige*, and *New World A-Comin'*—through all these phases, it is, or at least should have been, abundantly clear that here is one of the most gifted composers, in any category, of our day.

Duke Ellington.

137

Recording Information of Wax No. X-190

Date Recorded	6/21/26	By		At N Y.,

Subject (I'M JUST WILD ABOUT) ANIMAL CRACKERS   *Fox Trot*

By   DUKE ELLINGTON & HIS WASHINGTONIANS   Accompanied by

Composed by   RICH-GOSLOW & LINK   Music by

Words by   Published by HENRY WATERSON, INC.,

Copyright   19   Royalties

Recording Expense

Wax Shipped Copper Master-6/24/26   Trunk No.   Via

Suggest Using in   Supplement

Remarks

In the beginning there were the Washingtonians. Shown at the Kentucky Club in 1925 *(above photo)* are drummer Sonny Greer and *(standing, left to right)* Charlie Irvis, trombone; Elmer Snowden, banjo; Otto Hardwick, saxophone. Seated are "growl" trumpet star Bubber Miley *(left)* and Ellington. The card *(top)* is from one of Duke's earliest recording dates, for Gennett. The dim photo at the right shows some important additions made by 1929, including trombonists "Tricky Sam" Nanton *(left)* and Juan Tizol, with Cootie Williams, who replaced Miley, between them, and Johnny Hodges, at the right of the curtain.

The 1934 Ellington Orchestra, considered by many to be the Duke's greatest lineup. Saxes *(left to right)*: Hardwick, Harry Carney, Barney Bigard, Hodges. Trombones *(left to right)*: Nanton, Tizol, Lawrence Brown. Trumpets *(left to right)*: Rex Stewart, Williams, Arthur Whetsel. Besides Ellington and Greer, the rhythm section has Wellman Braud on bass, Fred Guy on guitar.

DUKE **ELLINGTON IN PERSON**
BROOKLYN PARAMOUNT
1,000 THRILLS "DR. JEKYLL & MR. HYDE" - YOU'LL NEVER FORGET IT
FREDRIC MARCH - MIRIAM HOPKINS IN SUPERB PERFORMANCES - IT'S EXCITING
GOTCHA - ON STAGE ALL COLORED SHOW - DUKE ELLINGTON & FAMOUS BAND

The marquee of the Brooklyn Paramount Theater speaks for itself. Below it is the mid-'30s reed section: "Toby" Hardwick *(front)* had been with the Duke since Washington days; Johnny Hodges *(left)* and Harry Carney *(right)* were from the Boston area, with the latter having joined the band in 1926, straight out of high school. Barney Bigard was New Orleans-born, a veteran of Chicago. The lower-left photo is of vocalist Ivie Anderson, who made a great many Ellington songs her special property. Beside her is a picture of the Duke as a resplendent young bandleader.

At the top, *the* trombone section. "Tricky Sam" *(left)* was a Harlem musician; Lawrence Brown *(right)* was from California; and Juan Tizol, from Puerto Rico, injected a Latin-American note into the band—and they formed a superb team. Below them, later photos of two great Ellington horns, Rex Stewart *(left)*, whose earlier career in Harlem is traced in Chapter 10; and Cootie Williams, from Alabama, strictly an open-horn stylist until he took over Bubber Miley's chair and produced a fine, muted "jungle" sound for more than a decade with the Duke.

Ben Webster.

Barney Bigard.

Otto Hardwick.

Harry Carney.

Johnny Hodges.

Ben Webster's impressive tenor sax was added in the late '30s, and these five continued on together into the '40s, creating that unique Ellington sound, one of the most remarkable units in jazz. Hodges and Webster are shown together at a late-'40s recording session, after both had left the Duke. (By 1955, Hodges was back in the fold; both he and Carney remained — apparently permanent fixtures—as of the mid-'60s.)

Hodges and Webster.

142

Sonny Greer and all his drums.

Ivie Anderson and Jimmy Blanton at a Colgate University concert.

A close-up of Blanton.

There was permanence: Sonny Greer was the only drummer from the start until the early 1950s. There was unavoidable change: Ivie Anderson, whose voice fitted so well the band's sound, left because of illness in 1942; Jimmy Blanton, who pointed the way for the "modern" melodic bass style, was on hand only in 1939-41, died of T.B. And when Cootie left in 1940, his replacement was the very jivey Ray Nance.

Trumpeter-violinist Ray Nance; he also sang.

143

An important 1942 change was the departure of Bigard, replaced by Jimmy Hamilton (*right*) who was to become another long-term member. Junior Raglin is the bassist; next to him, Ben Webster, who was soon to leave.

Among the changes of the mid-'40s was the addition of "Cat" Anderson, an impressive high-note man, to the trumpet section. Ray Nance is at his left, Shelton Hemphill at his right, in the photo just above. At the right, Duke goes over a score with Nance; swing-band veteran Taft Jordan, who joined in 1946, awaits his turn.

At the top of the page, a grouping that serves to remind that Ellington has always been one of the most inventive of arrangers. At his left is Billy Strayhorn, Duke's right-hand man, and a creator of rich melodies of his own; at his right, Sy Oliver, ace arranger for Jimmie Lunceford and Tommy Dorsey. Below that, the Duke with friends: Louis Armstrong and Strayhorn; and, in the right-hand picture, with French guitarist Django Reinhardt during a European tour.

A recording session of the early 1950s. The most notice-able change, undoubtedly, is the replacement of Sonny Greer by drummer Louis Bellson. Among other newcomers of that era: tenor sax Paul Gonsalves *(front row, left)* and Clark Terry *(far left in trumpet section)*.

On and on goes the Ellington story: by now the band is an American institution—something like the U.S. Senate, but with many fewer changes in personnel. The scene just above is a 1964 dance; Duke is shown with part of his reed section. Jimmy Hamilton *(left)* is the "newcomer," having arrived in '42; the returned Johnny Hodges first joined in 1928; Harry Carney has been on hand since '26! Clearly, there is as yet no way of summing up. Summations "are for dead men, aren't they?"—to borrow Duke's mild objection to publication of a biography in 1946. And Duke continues to shape and move his band in new directions and some well-established ones, continues to travel (to Asia and Japan now, as well as Europe), continues to re-

ceive awards. Perhaps he is past his creative peak, perhaps not. There also remains that intriguing, inevitable question that most probably can have no single answer: whether or not the startlingly versatile Ellington, besides being composer, arranger, leader, pianist, isn't also something of a hypnotist, expressing himself by thrusting greatness on the men who played the scores that, for the most part, he wrote. The evidence on one side notes that few who left the Duke have gone on to any notable jazz creativity. But on the other hand it's hard to deny the greatness inherent in that extraordinarily impressive roster of Ellington side-men, beginning with Miley, Nanton, Hodges, and con-tinuing to the present.

Kansas City Shuffle

IT'S NOT so much a Kansas City "style" as a capsule history of jazz in one town: from something close to New Orleans on to Swing, and beyond. It is a history that can be recounted in terms of a very few bands and key individuals—and of a special musical atmosphere that has always made this a musicians' town, a place where members of a traveling band could count on finding a challenging jam session in progress, where audiences were known to have more awareness and appreciation of good jazz than could consistently be hoped for in most other cities.

The story begins with the riverboats. Any geography book will quickly assure you that this town is not on the Mississippi River, but it *is* on the Missouri, and more than a few of the steamers turned west along that tributary from just above St. Louis to Kansas City. Before the 1920s the bands playing on those boats were, of course, spreading the sound of the original New Orleans music, and their hard-driving ensemble style struck fertile soil in Kansas City, which was almost ideally prepared to be a home for jazz. For this, some credit must be assigned to the celebrated Pendergast political machine, which for years helped make the town a symbol of just about all that was free-wheeling and wide-open. And there was more than just the New Orleans jazz influence: at roughly the time of the riverboats, the crude and rhythmic piano style to be known as boogie woogie had reached this area in its wanderings, and was to be heard in the local dives, establishing a tradition that remained there in the playing of men like Pete Johnson and that was clearly reflected in the pulsing beat of the Kansas City bands. Above all, this was a city with a large Negro population who supported several big ballrooms and dance halls and who wanted their dance music virile, with a strong, heavy beat.

Much of the story can be told entirely in terms of the band led by Bennie Moten, unquestioned leader among Kansas City groups from the time it was first formed in the early '20s. Their many recordings demonstrate an early allegiance to an almost "pure" traditional style, and then a gradual transition that eventually altered their sound substantially, making it far smoother and more swinging, but still driving and still with a pronounced feeling for the blues. In 1930, Moten just about completed the transition when he absorbed the nucleus of a young band that was carving out a name for itself in the Southwest. It was the Blue Devils of bassist Walter Page, including Count Basie, "Hot Lips" Page and the blues-shouting Jimmy Rushing. That was it, the foundation for what was to become, following Moten's death in the mid-'30s, that pillar of Swing, the Basie band.

There were others, too. George E. Lee's band, now forgotten, was once formidable competition for Moten. And Andy Kirk's a bit later, going through quite a bit of transition itself (in 1930, for example, they recorded King Oliver's *Snag It;* by 1936 they were doing *I'se a Muggin'*). And the Kansas City influence could be heard elsewhere, in a Harlem band of the late '20s like The Missourians, originally from the Midwest and heavily swayed by the Moten sound.

They had their own way of playing in Kansas City, their own beat, and the trumpets searing through the band sound, and the spirited repetitive riffs. Some argue that there is actually no specific Kansas City "style"; but no one can claim that this town wasn't a major jazz landmark.

Young Count Basie, with unidentified friends; from a mid-'20s photo.

The Bennie Moten band at its peak, in about 1929. Count Thamon Hayes (*fourth from left*) and Eddie Durham Basie, blues-shouter Jimmy Rushing (*standing*) and Mo- (*sixth from left*); saxophonists Harlan Leonard (*behind* ten are in the center. Others include trumpeters Hot Lips *Moten*) and Jack Washington (*second from right*); Buster Page (*left*) and Ed Lewis (*third from left*); trombonists Moten, accordion (*right*).

Just about the same Moten band, in 1931, on one of its favorite bandstands, at Kansas City's Fairyland Park.

Walter Page's Blue Devils, in Oklahoma City in about 1929. From this red-hot young group, Lips Page, Rushing and Durham came to Bennie Moten's orchestra. Tuba and bass man Walter Page joined them there later.

After Moten's death, Basie did not (according to his own story) *exactly* take over the band. He formed a group including several ex-Moten men; others went with this band, led by trombonist Thamon Hayes *(rear)*, including Ed Lewis *(left)*; saxophonists Woodie Walder *(fourth from right)* and Harlan Leonard *(third from right)*; Vernon Page, tuba *(right)*. Vic Dickenson *(fifth from right)* was also on trombone.

Andy Kirk's Twelve Clouds of Joy, in the top band photo, pose at a redecorated Fairyland Park dance pavilion, in 1935. Mary Lou Williams is in the center; saxes Dick Wilson and John Williams are fourth and second from the right; leader Kirk is at the far right. In the lower picture, taken in 1937, Kirk's is now one of the leading Swing bands, with Mary Lou, as pianist and arranger, still the key figure.

Mary Lou Williams.

Bill Basie, from Red Bank, New Jersey, made the Kansas City style his own and gave it to the whole country. The big break came when jazz enthusiast-critic-record executive John Hammond heard the band at the Reno Club; Basie followed up with the skill and the rhythmic surge. For the beat, credit the Count, bassist Walter Page, drummer Jo Jones, guitarist Freddie Green, all shown in the top picture. That photo is of the band in the spring of 1940, in Chicago. The saxes are *(left to right)* Buddy Tate, Tab Smith, Jack Washington, Lester Young, and on trombone are *(left to right)* Vic Dickenson, Dicky Wells, Dan Minor. In the earlier lower photo, Benny Morton is the trombonist on the left; Young is readily identifiable on the right by the horn held sideways. There is, of course, no end in sight for Basie (a portion of the next chapter picks up the story), as his band has gone on driving well into the 1960s.

153

15

Swing, Brother, Swing

FIRST IT WAS Benny Goodman, then it was everyone, and the kids jitterbugging in the theater aisles. Among other things, though hardly most important, it was the first time that outsiders began to concern themselves about the sociological and psychological implications of jazz (*Why* did everyone flock around the bandstands? *What* made those 'teen-age dancers carry on like that?). Swing provoked a pretty extreme set of reactions, it's true, but one big reason it was all so noticeable was that this was the first time a form of jazz had the whole broad sweep of the country, rather than any one limited area, as its base of operations.

It couldn't have happened—at least not on so massive a scale—before the days of coast-to-coast radio networks (it was the "Camel Caravan" broadcasts as much as anything else that first put the Goodman band across). And it remained on a nation-wide level through the half-dozen or more years that were the life span of the Swing craze, years that for all the many orchestras involved were a mad race of recording, radio shows, theater dates, college proms, hotel dates, and never-ending strings of one-night stands.

Swing had been building up, far from quietly, for some time before Benny and his talented co-workers brought it to the surface when he bowled them over at the Palomar Ballroom in Los Angeles in 1935 and then at the Congress Hotel in Chicago. Goodman was to stay on top throughout, indicating it was no fluke that he was the one to get the first big break. And in any case, it turned out to be everyone's big break. The panic was on, and the money started rolling in for countless bands, most of which turn up on the following pages.

In a sense, Swing effectively combined some key

virtues of its big-band predecessors. Many of the musical mannerisms of the Negro bands were adopted by the white leaders, and their most brilliant arrangers were often adopted, too. Goodman set the pace here as well, by the extremely astute move of hiring Fletcher Henderson to create the foundations of his "book." The technique of being able to double as a smooth, sweet dance band was carried over from the Whiteman era, where it had worked so well. Actually, it was more the Ben Pollack concept that was used; as in the band in which Goodman had begun his career, the personnel were primarily jazz-oriented musicians, and there was much emphasis on hot solos by these men. Indeed, one of the major phenomena of Swing was that sidemen became stars in their own right: names like Bunny Berigan, Gene Krupa, Harry James, Ziggy Elman, Lionel Hampton and many more were almost as close to being household words as the names of the bandleaders.

It wasn't all big-band music, either. New York's 52nd Street and its counterparts in other large cities produced their own free and loose brand of Swing, which was echoed in the small units set up within many big bands (Goodman's Trio, Quartet, Sextet; Tommy Dorsey's Clambake Seven), and in the innumerable groups whipped up for recording sessions.

All this was undoubtedly very much a product of the times: a nation staggering out of the Big Depression, pre-war jitters, Repeal. But whatever the reasons, it rocked and leaped from coast to coast, it grabbed hold of more people, certainly, than any other jazz style before or since, it turned bandleaders into celebrities as fan-worshipped as any movie star, and it turned jazz, for once, into a happily successful big business.

Benny Goodman, in the mid-1930s.

An immediate predecessor of Swing was Glen Gray's Casa Loma Orchestra, shown here as it opened at the Glen Island Casino, near New York (later a celebrated haven for Swing bands), in the Spring of 1931. Trumpeter Sunny Dunham is at the far left, Gray is the second saxophonist from the right.

The Bob Crosby band came into existence in 1935, with its nucleus a group of former Ben Pollack sidemen, and played its brand of Dixieland tempered with Swing (or vice versa) right from the start. Among the original personnel lined up here in their neat white shoes are guitarist Nappy Lamare *(second from left)*, sax men Eddie Miller *(third from left)* and Gil Rodin *(second from right)*, drummer Ray Bauduc *(fourth from left)*. Crosby is in the center, with dark jacket. Trumpeter Yank Lawson towers at his left, bass player Bob Haggart at his right.

The Dorsey Brothers had had an orchestra, off and on, since 1928, and all that kept their 1934-35 group from being called a Swing band was that the term wasn't in use yet. By the time it was, the brothers had had their 1935 split-up and gone their separate ways. In the round-the-table photo above, Tommy and Jimmy stand over their vocalist, Kay Weber; Glenn Miller sits at her left; drummer Ray McKinley *(front, right)* has his back to the camera. In the lower, at-work picture, vocalist Bob Crosby is also on hand *(left foreground)*, this being just before he formed his own band.

This is the official opening of the Swing Era. Benny Goodman's Orchestra, 1936, with a rhythm section of Jess Stacy, Gene Krupa, Harry Goodman on bass, Allan Reuss on guitar, and including a couple of sidemen who were to be long-time fixtures in Benny's sections, trumpeter Gordon "Chris" Griffin *(third from left)* and trombonist Red Ballard, who stands behind Krupa. The photo of Goodman with his first vocalist, Helen Ward, is probably *not* intended to prove that, after having been with Benny since his late-1934 broadcasting-studio band, she could now, at long last, afford a fur coat.

Tommy Dorsey had his own band now, and in 1936 was not too far behind Goodman. It's somewhat strange to note that the line-up included two Austin High Chicago-ans, drummer Dave Tough and Bud Freeman, tenor sax, who is behind vocalist Edythe Wright. Also on hand is trumpeter Max Kaminsky, at Tough's right.

Count Basie's band was also among the earlier Swing successes, as noted in the previous chapter. This was the sax section in 1937-38, with the emphasis on Herschel Evans *(left)* and Lester Young *(right)*. Star trumpeter Buck Clayton is seated at the left of guitarist Freddy Green on this crowded 52nd Street bandstand.

On the next few pages, several of the many bands that rose to prominence during the late '30s. Leaders Charlie Barnet *(top photo)* and Jimmy Dorsey *(lower photo)* both played saxophone, but resemblances end there. Barnet, an admirer of Duke Ellington, kept his band's jazz quotient high, from the days of *Cherokee* through his use of modernists like Neal Hefti and Buddy de Franco in the early '40s. Dorsey, although he featured a Dixieland unit in later years, depended most heavily on star vocalists Helen O'Connell and Bob Eberle. These groups and the Herman band on the facing page, happen to be shown in the same place: the Panther Room—note the spotted upholstery—of Chicago's Hotel Sherman.

Another prominent group was the "Band That Plays the Blues" developed by Woody Herman after taking over from Isham Jones when that dance-band leader retired in 1936. They did offer more than a fair share of blues-tinged jazz, with a driving beat set down by pianist Tommy Linehan, drummer Frank Carlson, Walter Yoder on bass, Hy White on guitar.

Jimmie Lunceford's powerhouse crew first scored at the Cotton Club in 1934, kept on top on into the '40s. Lunceford waved a baton, and the stars were Sy Oliver (*front row, left*) both on trumpet and as arranger, alto sax man Willie Smith (*front row, fifth from left*), trombonist Trummy Young (*second from left*), and drummer Jimmy Crawford.

Among the several Negro bands that flourished during the Swing Era were two using "E.H." on their music stands. Erskine Hawkins came up from Alabama in the mid-'30s with the nucleus of his band. He was a flashy trumpeter, but the group behind him was a soundly swinging one, most notably tenor sax man Paul Bascombe. The Earl Hines band, featuring the leader's leaping piano, grew increasingly "modern" in approach, but the veteran clarinet and saxophone star Omer Simeon *(front row, center)* was with them until 1940.

Chick Webb discovered Ella Fitzgerald at an amateur night at Harlem's Apollo Theater in 1934. Ella, shown here on the stage of the New York Paramount, helped to keep the drummer's band at the top right up until his death in 1939.

Lucky Millinder's was, particularly in the very early 1940s, a mightily swinging group, with the aid of such as saxophonist Tab Smith *(front row, center)* and the rocking vocals of Sister Rosetta Tharpe (not shown).

Cab Calloway's fame came from his jivey antics. His band's musical qualities stemmed from the ex-Missourians in the early days, and by the late '30s from such as bassist Milt Hinton, pianist Benny Payne, Danny Barker on guitar, Tyree Glenn *(right)* on trombone—and above all, from slim drummer Cozy Cole and the stocky, rich-toned sax man, Chu Berry.

Cozy and Chu.

After the quick run-through on the preceding pages, it seems time for a more detailed retrospective look at some of the major bands and personalities of these fabulous years. On this page begins the Benny Goodman saga, with views of some of the reasons for his almost incredible early popularity. Benny is shown with *the* trumpet section, which worked as a unit continuously from the end of 1936 through the end of 1938: *(left to right)* Chris Griffin, Ziggy Elman, Harry James. Below them is Martha Tilton, the band's vocalist during just about the same period.

164

Goodman may or may not have originated the idea of the small hot unit within the larger band. He most certainly nurtured the idea and made it something of great musical value. The Goodman Trio is almost as old as the band itself, and when Lionel Hampton joined the band, it became the Quartet. Although both Hamp and pianist Teddy Wilson worked primarily in the special unit, any use of Negroes in a big white band that toured the plusher location spots of the nation was clearly a victory for good music over prejudice.

Gene Krupa.

Teddy Wilson.

Lionel Hampton.

Naturally enough, there were constant shifts of personnel. The 1939 band is shown, in the top photo, waiting for the ferry to Santa Catalina Island, California. Among those present: vocalist Helen Forrest, flanked by Benny and his brother Irving; bassist Artie Bernstein; pianist Johnny Guarnieri *(crouching, left)*; saxophonist Toots Mondello *(crouching, center)*; drummer Nick Fatool, at Benny's left; Ziggy Elman *(right)*. In the more customary indoor setting, an early 1941 band, with Dave Tough, drums; huge trumpeter Jimmy Maxwell and Irving Goodman still on hand; Lou McGarity and Cutty Cutshall *(right)*, trombones; Mike Bryan, guitar, with sax man Georgie Auld at his left.

Goodman with the man he has always credited, quite justly, with providing a very large share of the bedrock on which Benny's early bands stood. Fletcher Hender- son's arrangements, some based on what his own band had played, were as good a working definition as you could hope to find of what Swing is all about.

By 1941, Goodman went so far as to put a mixed band on the stand. Drummer Catlett and bassist John Simmons were with him only briefly, but Cootie Williams, who had just ended his long stay with Ellington, stayed for over a year. Others in this band are Vido Musso, who stands at the left of the sax section; Billy Butterfield, second trumpeter from the left, and the brilliant new pianist, Mel Powell. In the lower photo, Cootie waits while Benny takes a solo on one of the many Sextet numbers that featured the Williams horn.

Charlie Christian, shown here jamming with a group that includes Teddy Wilson, had joined Goodman in 1939. By 1941 illness had him out of the band as often as in; then he left altogether; in 1942 he died, aged 24. Christian, born in Oklahoma, played an advanced solo-style guitar from the start, was among the experimenters in be-bop at Minton's (see Chapter 19), and in his few years influenced the whole new trend in guitar playing.

Vido Musso (*center*) and Toots Mondello added considerably to Goodman's later sax sections.

A mutual admiration society: Count Basie appears on several Goodman sextet recordings.

Mel Powell, a key man in the early-'40s, had begun as a very young devotee of Dixieland, but very soon changed his allegiance.

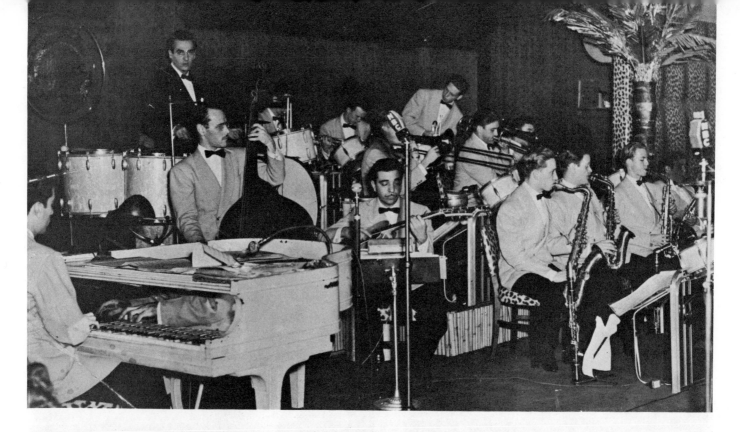

Before the heyday of Swing, sidemen had been nearly-anonymous craftsmen. Now they were heavily publicized stars, with the fans after their autographs as well as the leader's. Inevitably, the most celebrated took off on their own. By 1938, Gene Krupa *(upper photo)* had begun his career as a bandleader; within the year there was also a Harry James Orchestra. These two former Goodman-ites were clearly the most successful at this branching-out. In both pictures, the scene is once again the Panther Room in Chicago.

Tommy Dorsey was, on the whole, Goodman's chief rival. Bunny Berigan, perhaps the most talented trumpet man of this era, was with T.D. only briefly, in 1937. But his work included the memorable recordings of *Marie* and *Song of India,* so that in retrospect he remains permanently associated with the band. The lower photo shows Dorsey and his sax section on-stage at the mecca of all Swing bands, New York's Paramount Theater, home base for the wildest of the jitterbugs, in 1937.

Buddy Rich.

In the upper photo is a classic (if not necessarily permanent) reconciliation scene of the late '30s. Goodman and Dorsey, or at least their press agents, had been feuding a bit, as was then the custom. Here all seems well again. Just above: Dorsey's band of the early '40s. It went in at times for trimmings, like this string section and harpist, more in keeping with Tommy's billing as "The Sentimental·Gentleman of Swing" than with jazz. But, from the end of 1939 on, he continued to feature the dynamic drumming of Buddy Rich, which very often more than compensated.

172

Another major attraction, at least as far as the bobby-soxers were concerned, was young Frank Sinatra. Fresh from his first band job (with Harry James), the singer joined Dorsey in 1940.

A study in the passage of time: The picture on the left was taken at the beginning of 1939. The one directly below dates from 1954. Dorsey was then still very much an active performer (his death, in '56, was accidental), but the photo indicates graphically just how much time had gone by since Swing was young.

Bob Crosby's band offered a unique mixture of swing, sweet ballads and a brand of Dixieland often not too far removed from traditional jazz. The 1937 edition of the Bob Cats, the Dixieland unit, is shown *(below)* inside the circular bar at New York's Hickory House. On hand are *(left to right)* Ray Bauduc, Yank Lawson, Warren Smith, Matty Matlock, Eddie Miller, Bob Haggart, Bob Zurke, Nappy Lamare. All of them are in the full-band picture, which also shows trumpeters Charlie Spivak *(right)* and Billy Butterfield, and sax man Gil Rodin, at Crosby's left, a veteran of the first Ben Pollack band.

174

Bob Haggart and Ray Bauduc—the full personnel of the celebrated recording of *Big Noise from Winnetka.*

Chicagoan Joe Sullivan *(left),* snapped on the Atlantic City boardwalk with Bauduc, was the group's piano man in 1939, helped keep the jazz level of the Crosby band high.

From 1940 on, it was Jess Stacy on piano, veteran of the Chicago style and of the original Goodman band.

Irving Fazola, who joined Crosby in 1938, was from New Orleans and played in the great clarinet tradition of that city.

Artie Shaw had been trying hard, and interestingly, since 1936, but didn't really make the grade until *Begin the Beguine* became a hit record late in 1938. Then his rise was rapid enough for this New York marquee to bill him as "1939 New King of Swing." Shortly thereafter, the unpredictable Mr. Shaw (who was to gather as much publicity for his several marriages—Lana Turner and Ava Gardner being among the ex-Mrs. Shaws—as for anything else) renounced the band business "permanently," with a blast at the jitterbugs.

Hot Lips Page.

Roy Eldridge.

Before too many months of 1940 were gone, Shaw was back from retirement, with bands that included string sections, but also some top-flight jazz artists. At the top are two stars with whom he breached the color line: Page in his 1941 band, Eldridge in the group organized late in World War II. The '40 and '41 units also featured two men shown in the center photo, saxophonist Georgie Auld *(right)* and Jack Jenney, trombone *(rear, right)*. During part of the war period, Shaw led one of the best-known service bands.

Glenn Miller had been in jazz since the Ben Pollack band was formed, and on the early Swing scene with the Dorsey Brothers, but it was as late as 1939 before he led a successful band of his own. His success then was most thoroughgoing. His was one of the smoothest and most danceable of bands. It was also apparently a good school: trumpet men Billy May and Ray Anthony and saxophonist Hal McIntyre all became top post-war bandleaders.

Ray McKinley.

Tex Beneke.

Two of the men most closely linked with Miller are shown above. Beneke played and sang with the band from the start, but McKinley was never with a civilian Miller orchestra. He was part of the Army Air Force band formed when Glenn became Captain Miller in 1942. In this mass photo, McKinley is sprawled in the front row *(second from right)*. Among the many other Swing sidemen on hand, pianist Mel Powell *(front, right)*; clarinetist Peanuts Hucko *(front, fourth from right)*. Miller was lost on a plane flight over the English channel. After the war, both Beneke and McKinley organized groups in the Miller vein.

All through the era, there was Count Basie's band with its surging Kansas City beat, blasting out perhaps the finest jazz of all. A November, 1940, recording session for Columbia, shortly before Lester Young ended his five-year stay with the Count, offers just about their classic lineup (*all listed left to right*). Trumpets: Buck Clayton, Ed Lewis, Al Killian, Harry Edison. Trombones: Vic Dickenson, Dicky Wells, Dan Minor. Saxes: Young, Jack Washington, Earl Warren, Buddy Tate. Rhythm section: as always (see page 182). *Left*, it's "Mr. Five by Five," Jimmy Rushing, an original Basie-ite, in action on-stage.

This ranks as a rare Lester Young picture, since his sax is *not* held at a forty-five-or-more-degree angle. Lester is said to have joined Basie by sending him a telegram: he'd heard a broadcast from the Reno Club, in Kansas City, in 1935, and decided the band needed a tenor man. Basie could hardly have done better than Young, one of the truly great saxophonists. His lighter, harder tone was revolutionary in a generation dominated by Coleman Hawkins' rich sound; thus he is credited as a direct predecessor and inspirer of the modernists.

Herschel Evans died in the early days of Basie's success, and now remains a memory compounded of his impressive work on pre-1939 records and stories of his after-hours musical battles with Young.

The Kansas City pattern called for a trumpet soloist with power and clarity, capable of riding hot and high over the full-band sound without growing raucous. Buck Clayton filled that role with distinction for almost a decade.

This is what was known as Basie's "All-American Rhythm Section." They came out of Kansas City as a unit, and remained a perfectly meshed team on into the late '40s: Bill Basie, with his few-notes piano style; Freddy Green, guitar; Jo Jones, drums; and—above all—the rock-solid bass player, Walter Page.

Long after the Swing craze was a thing of the past, Basie continued as leader of a top-rated band, adding a share of the new sounds of the '40s and '50s, but remaining a master of "swing." His 1955 group, a totally revamped one, included Joe Newman (*rear row, left*), trumpet; saxophonists Frank Foster (*front row, fourth from left*) and Frank Wess (*front row, right*). An added footnote: in the mid-'60s, with many more personnel changes, Basie was still swinging.

"All star" bands were a standard Swing Era device, reflecting public taste as indicated via *Metronome* magazine polls. The upper photo shows some of the 1940 winners at their special recording date. It's *(left to right)* Ziggy Elman and Cootie Williams on trumpet; trombonists J. C. Higginbotham and Tommy Dorsey; Benny Goodman on clarinet; Tex Beneke, Benny Carter, Toots Mondello, Coleman Hawkins as the sax section. Buddy Rich is the drummer. In the lower photo, the previous year's winners, including Charlie Barnet *(left)* and Jack Teagarden, who is standing behind Goodman, listen to a recording being played back.

Much of the vast amount of small-band activity connected with Swing involved ever-shifting personnel, but John Kirby's band remained constant, dispensing a unique brand of integrated ultra-smooth jazz. Left to right, it's Billy Kyle, Kirby, Russell Procope, Buster Bailey (these last three all Fletcher Henderson alumni), Charlie Shavers, drummer O'Neil Spencer.

Teddy Wilson, a "name" after his Benny Goodman days, led various small units. This 1940 group had (left to right) George James, baritone sax; Wilson; Jimmy Hamilton, clarinet; Bill Coleman, trumpet; Benny Morton, trombone; J. C. Heard, drums; Al Hall, bass.

A notable partnership was that of Red Allen, the hard-blasting trumpeter, and trombonist J. C. Higginbotham, dating from 1929, when they had been together in the Luis Russell band. In the upper photo they are backing Billie Holiday; the year is 1939, a time when Red and Higgy were often to be found on New York's "Swing Street"—52nd Street. Another familiar figure on that block was trumpeter Frankie Newton, shown in the lower picture on the bandstand at Kelly's Stable. His clarinetist, more famous in later years as a tenor sax man with Woody Herman, is Joe "Flip" Phillips.

Featuring
ADELE GIRARD

Now Playing
Hickory House
N.Y.C.

JOE MARSALA

There might be some argument about the preciseness of classifying the men on this page as Swing musicians. It's true that they can be taken as forerunners of the latter-day Dixieland detailed in the next chapter, but it is equally true that all were major 52nd Street attractions during the late '30s, Wingy Manone in particular having done much to create "Swing Street" during a long 1935 run at the Hickory House. The point undoubtedly is that nomenclature didn't concern them in the slightest. Clarinetist Marsala's Chicagoans are his brother Marty on trumpet; his wife Adele, harp; Carmen Mastren, guitar; Artie Shapiro, bass; Danny Alvin, drums; Joe Bushkin, piano.

Wingy Manone, 1938.

Bobby Hackett, 1939.

Stuff Smith, one of the jiviest.

In small clubs on New York's Swing Street, in Chicago's Loop, in Hollywood, and all way stops, there were small and swinging units showcasing such talent as the always-great Coleman Hawkins *(left)*, or the ebullient altoist Pete Brown (shown with trumpeter Bill Coleman).

In 1939, young Nat "King" Cole's trio (with Oscar Moore on guitar, Wesley Prince on bass), was among the promising jazz acts on the Western club circuit, featuring Cole's vocals and Earl Hines-influenced piano style.

"Lady Day"—at the left, Billie Holiday in the early '40s, with the inevitable gardenia. Below, a decade later.

These are two of the very best, best-known, most influential, and most copied of singers. Ella Fitzgerald (*right*) fronted the band of her "discoverer," Chick Webb, for a short time after his death. Then she took off on her own on an unswerving path to the top, to become unquestioned queen of jazz vocalists for many, many years—in the opinion of public and fellow professionals alike. Billie Holiday first made her mark through a series of late-1930s recordings with small groups led by Teddy Wilson. A highly effective, if highly stylized, artist, she eventually succumbed in 1959 to the end result of personal problems rivaling those of any of the girls in her sad songs.

Lee Wiley has been a notable singer of popular "standards" and the better show tunes for a long time, always with considerable jazz feeling and warmth, and with the collaboration of men like the two shown here with her at a late-'30s recording session, Max Kaminsky and Joe Bushkin.

Mildred Bailey, the Rocking Chair Lady and wife of vibraphonist Red Norvo, made her start with the Paul Whiteman orchestra in 1931. In the next two decades (she died in 1951) she worked and recorded with virtually every top jazzman of the day—testimony enough to her colleagues' appreciation of her rich voice and impeccable beat.

Art Tatum.

Jack Teagarden.

Finally, two figures of the period who are rather hard to classify: Tatum simply because, as the outstanding solo pianist of the day, he made his own category, rather than f tting into anyone else's. A brilliant technician, Art has been called ornate by some, a genius by many more. Jack Teagarden, the Texas boy who played with the Pollack band and was influenced by the Harlem bands, is almost too varied to pin down. At different moments of the era, he was to be found playing small-band Swing, Dixieland, or leading his own big band, in addition to all of which he remained a fine blues-style singer.

Benny Goodman, as he looked in the mid-'30s, was a logical opening for this chapter. Similarly, Goodman in the '50s, as shown above, is a logical closing. Swing itself, as a feverish, all-pervading fad, is of course gone. It might have burned itself out in time, but actually its end was hastened by World War II: the draft, travel restrictions and the like made the big, traveling bands unfeasible. By the time the war ended, the music business was emphasizing individual vocalists (representing less of an investment risk) and jazz had turned in other directions. But Goodman himself retained his personal prestige and drawing power for many years. He has made more than one successful, if brief, return to action: organizing a band for a State Department tour of the Far East in 1956, and another for the Brussels World's Fair in '58, among others. By the '60s, however, Benny and Swing itself were largely limited to occasional token reunion-type appearances—plus some traveling bands that still carried the names of such as the late Dorsey brothers and Glenn Miller. In short, nostalgia was by that time the main drawing card.

At the Jazz Band Ball

EDDIE CONDON and what he called his "barefoot mob" of transplanted Chicagoans turned the trick for the most part, with jam sessions and concerts, and finally took up permanent residence in Greenwich Village, making their latter-day Dixieland a leading staple item on the New York scene in the '40s and '50s.

It was rather amazing how this man cast his shadow so large across a whole phase of jazz while spending so little time on the bandstand. No reflection on Mr. Condon, who seems always to have been an impresario at heart and too restless a type really to enjoy sitting down and quietly playing a guitar. If Eddie spent a lot of time off the stand, he spent it being master of ceremonies at jazz concerts and radio and TV broadcasts, and in running the club bearing his name. His picture was on the cover of *Time* magazine, suggesting that he might be regarded as a symbol (although Eddie, being completely flesh and blood, might not approve of that concept). He succeeded in becoming the representative of the whole style in the minds of a great many people, providing a concrete mental picture that made the music readily identifiable, and this worked out just fine. For by doing so he secured for this form of jazz a large and faithful audience that for many years gave it a kind of stability and apparent permanence that few other forms (perhaps only the music of Storyville, in its day) had achieved.

A good many of the faces on the following pages are the very same, although a bit older, as those encountered in Chapter 8. But these Chicagoans, so-called, actually spent comparatively few years playing in their home town. They were in and out of New York for several years and finally, in about the middle '30s, they made it their headquarters. In those depression days clubs were apt to be shuttered and steady jobs few (except for the handful of musicians who were both able and willing to fit into big Swing bands). So, some place along the line, that informal, after-hours, for-musicians-only gathering known as the "jam session" was converted into a public institution and a livelihood. At night clubs that needed an off-evening shot in the arm, and then with increasing frequency on the stage of staid Town Hall, casually shifting groups played the jazz standards. (It was basically a white personnel, although actually the color line was breached here more quickly and lastingly than ever before.) Inevitably, this kind of playing had a permanent effect on their style: the repertoire had to remain unchanging, the ensemble portions formalized, the primary emphasis on solos, so that any or all of them could fit into a given band at any time.

Describing this style as Dixieland makes it at least the third to bear this confusingly over-used name. The three are closely enough linked, though. In a sense, it's a neat rejoining of a pattern that began with early white New Orleans jazz: the Original Dixieland Jazz Band was a strong influence on the Red Nichols-Miff Mole crowd, who were the first New York Dixielanders. The New Orleans Rhythm Kings contributed greatly to the initial musical education of the Chicagoans. And it all meshed together into a music that, even though it has over the years become rather static, is strictly and solidly professional, never less than highly competent, and to a great many people still capable of being among the most exciting and stimulating of all jazz forms.

Eddie Condon.

There was a gradual gathering, in the East, of the clan. The photograph is supposedly taken at a "backstage jam session" at Boston's Symphony Hall, dubious wording which leads to a slight suspicion that it was specially posed. Nonetheless it significantly brings together Tommy Dorsey, Louis Armstrong, bass player Pops Foster (*standing, center*), trumpeter Red Allen (*right*) and three transplanted Chicagoans, Bud Freeman, Eddie Condon, George Wettling. The poster announces the New York opening of a band including Freeman, Condon, Pee Wee Russell, Max Kaminsky and Dave Tough, in 1940.

The upper picture is of perhaps the greatest recording band of the later-Dixieland style: Muggsy Spanier and His Ragtime Band. Spanier and George Brunies, emerging from their stay with Ted Lewis, joined with clarinetist Rod Cless and a varying rhythm section (Bob Casey, bass, and Marty Greenberg, drums, are shown here) to make sixteen memorable versions of jazz standards for the Blue Bird label in 1939. At the right are Frankie Newton, George Wettling and Mezz Mezzrow during a recording session.

Nick's was a roomy Greenwich Village restaurant that noted its "Sizzling Steaks" in neon outside, but was far more widely known for its music from the late 1930s until the early 1960s. It briefly featured Negro traditionalists like those pictured here: Sidney Bechet *(left)*, bassist Wellman Braud, drummer Zutty Singleton, but soon became the stamping grounds of the Dixielanders. The early band shown below offers the trombone of George Brunies, the clarinet of Pee Wee Russell, and a rear view of trumpeter Bobby Hackett.

In the post-war period, Muggsy Spanier settled in New York, while Miff Mole, veteran of an early local small-band style, brought his trombone back onto the scene. Pee Wee Russell seemed almost as permanent a part of the picture as the unchanging decor; only the moustache was variable. Gene Schroeder on piano was another regular at Nick's. The club became so synonymous with the music that there were some who, rather coyly, referred to it as "Nicksieland jazz." (There really was a Nick, too: Nick Rongetti, who loved to join the intermission pianist, and kept an extra piano in front of the bandstand for that purpose.) For those who consider *this* music corny, let it be noted that when Nick's closed, it was replaced by one of those clubs that feature all-banjo bands and fake handlebar moustaches.

Large-scale jam sessions on-stage, known thereafter as concerts, were organized by Eddie Condon in the early '40s. They packed New York's Town Hall regularly, with some sessions broadcast. Here some men play, others wait or wander, and still others are waiting backstage. Condon, sometimes at the microphone *(right)*, as he is here, and sometimes facing the audience over the back of that chair at the center, was at the start of his impresario's career. And there's little or nothing on those music stands.

197

Studies of three key figures with faces made to order for the camera: Muggsy Spanier *(above)*, who could surely be taken for an ex-prizefighter; Pee Wee Russell *(left)*, with the appearance of a sad clown, a man who has been described as "looking like the sort you have to tell anecdotes about"; Wild Bill Davison *(on facing page)*, looking as brash and buoyant as his sound, with his cornet invariably seeming to be jutting at an angle from the corner of his mouth.

There were always new clubs, though often only temporarily: 101st Street is far afield in New York, but in 1940 pianist Art Hodes, Rod Cless and George Brunies held forth for a while there *(upper photo)* at a branch of a local restaurant chain. The lower picture is the Pied Piper, a Greenwich Village spot that flourished during the war years. This is in 1944: Cless, Bob Haggart on bass, Max Kaminsky on trumpet, Frank Orchard on trombone, with regular pianist James P. Johnson seated at a table *(right)*.

Jimmy Ryan's was the home of the most celebrated of the organized jam sessions. The postcard announces the lineup for one 1943 event. Ryan's was durable enough to survive successive waves of boppers and strip girls in the surrounding 52nd Street clubs; finally evicted in 1962 by skyscraper builders, it moved two blocks and continued to offer Dixieland. A late-'40s lineup (*above*) fea-tured Max Kaminsky and his felt mute, with Cecil Scott on clarinet, Arthur Trappier, drums, and Dick Carey on piano. In 1954 and 1955 (*below*) the de Paris brothers held forth: Wilbur on trombone, Sidney on trumpet; with Omer Simeon, clarinet; Don Kirkpatrick, piano; Eddie Gibbs, banjo; Freddie Moore, drums.

Beginning in the late 1940s, there sprang up in New York what was to become a regular weekend crowd-puller, and can only be described as a combination of concert, jam session and dance, held at barn-like halls on lower Second Avenue. These pictures, taken at Stuyvesant Casino, suggest just how strange and crowded the usual lineups could be. *Above:* Ray McKinley, drums; Lou McGarity, trombone; Lee Castle, trumpet; Pee Wee Russell. *Below (from the left):* Buster Bailey, Vic Dickenson, Wilbur de Paris, Omer Simeon; with Lips Page and Rex Stewart at the right.

Recording was a particularly important and varied activity in this period. *Above:* a 1944 Blue Note rehearsal, with *(rear)* Sid Jacobs, bass; Danny Alvin, drums; and *(left to right)* Rod Cless, guitarist Jack Bland, trombonist Ray Conniff, Max Kaminsky, and Art Hodes. *Left:* a celebrated 1944 date entirely devoted to doing *A Good Man Is Hard to Find*. Most clearly visible is the rhythm section: Artie Shapiro on bass, Eddie Condon, Jess Stacy, George Wettling. The label, Commodore, was an offshoot of New York's Commodore Music Shop, which in the late '30s and early '40s was close to a second home for jazz musicians and fans.

On these two pages, a picture gallery of some New York-Dixieland notables of the 1940s and '50s.

Jimmy McPartland.

Bud Freeman.

George Wettling.

Albert Nicholas.

Edmond Hall.

Ralph Sutton at the piano.

Joe Sullivan and "blue-blower" Red McKenzie.

Dave Tough.

Under the striped canopy overhanging the bandstand at the Greenwich Village club known as Eddie Condon's *(above)*. The time: opening night, in 1946. The visible cast *(left to right):* Condon, Gene Schroeder, Joe Marsala, Bud Freeman, Bill Davison, Brad Gowans. The club flourished for a decade, then literally disappeared as progress (i.e.; big-building construction) rolled on. Relocated in midtown New York, the new Eddie Condon's serves, in the picture below, as setting for a mid-'60s reunion of George Brunis *(left)* and Tony Parenti (once of New Orleans), and Bobby Hackett *(right).*

"Reunion" and nostalgia is inevitably and increasingly the focal point as the years move on for the one-time swashbucklers of Chicago and New York "Dixieland." This chapter closes (on the facing page) with last views of Jack Teagarden, who died in 1964, together with Bud Freeman, Pee Wee Russell, and cornetist Jimmy McPartland, at rehearsals for one of those catch-all TV jazz specials. But it seems important to note that there is more than just nostalgia on display here. Those pictures also show us some of the most vital and important talents in all the story of jazz.

206

17

Come Back, Sweet Papa

THEY BOUGHT Bunk Johnson a new set of teeth and a horn, and coaxed Kid Ory away from the chicken farm, and the old-timers blasted away as good as new, offering an effective if rather unexpected kind of proof that theirs was a long-lived and still exciting music.

These two, above all, were the major figures of the wave of "rediscovery"—plucked out of obscurity to recreate with really astounding vigor the jazz of their youth. In the intervening years, a great many sweeping changes in jazz had come and gone. Many of the early musicians were dead and more were forgotten. Thus it was rather startling when these two very live ghosts from a legendary past appeared on the scene and proceeded to make the shadows into substance, to put flesh on the dim legends. They re-affirmed the early jazz traditions in the best and simplest way possible—by demonstrating how much of the old drive and skill they had retained and how thoroughly it could, after all those years, capture an audience.

The finding of Bunk came first, in 1938, when the editors of the book, *Jazzmen*, Frederic Ramsey, Jr., and Charles Edward Smith, followed up Louis Armstrong's suggestion that Johnson could probably give them information of interest about the old days and could probably be found in New Iberia, Louisiana. After that, several others were located, too, as jazz writers and enthusiasts came to the sudden realization that more than a few New Orleans veterans were still alive. It may seem now to have been a somewhat ironical situation: the musicians had not, of course, done anything to keep their existence secret and most of the men who were "found" were not aware that they had been lost. They had been playing in

New Orleans or elsewhere for a good many years, making a meager living at it, or maybe they had become stevedores or Pullman porters or farmhands and just about forgotten that they were supposed to be jazz immortals. But it must be recalled that documentation of early jazz was a brand-new idea in the late '30s; no one had really thought in terms of researching for people. But the discovery of Bunk touched off the spark, and they began to turn up both old-timers and what might be called middle-timers (musicians like George Lewis, belonging to a post-Storyville generation, who had unobtrusively continued to play traditional-style jazz for New Orleans Negro audiences). The jazz public owed a considerable debt to the handful of jazz writers—Gene Williams, Bill Russell, Ralph Gleason and others—who bestirred themselves to go out and find these memorable figures from what seemed a remote past.

At first, the intention seemed only to gather their stories. Then in 1940, some recordings were made of a band led by Kid Rena, who had been in the Waifs' Home with Louis Armstrong, and including Alphonse Picou, credited with creating the classic clarinet solo on *High Society*. After that there was considerable recording and playing. It is certainly dangerous to bring back figures of legend, well past their prime, and expose them to the harsh light of reality. But things worked out remarkably well. Some few, like Ory, seemed as good as they'd ever been. Bunk was on occasions quite magnificent, and even when he faltered, the combination of what he was trying to play and the overwhelming aura of nostalgia and romance felt by his audiences was enough to make it quite clear that this particular noble experiment had been a most valuable one.

Bunk Johnson.

In a very real sense, the "rediscovery" of the forgotten jazz giants of an earlier day began with three 1938 recording sessions organized by French jazz Critic Hugues Panassie *(standing, center)*, featuring New Orleans-born Tommy Ladnier *(right)*. The records, on which Mezz Mezzrow *(left)*, James P. Johnson *(seated)* and Sidney Bechet also played, did much to spark the veteran Bechet's return to prominence. They might also have helped Ladnier, but he died of a heart attack only a few months after they were released.

Sidney Bechet.

210

Although the great days were no more than old memories, or perhaps just stories from their childhood, New Orleans musicians like these marched and played in the old brass band tradition.

Many of the old-line musicians had drifted away. In this 1941 snapshot, Sidney Bechet talks with clarinetist George Baquet, who had been leading a small, obscure band in Philadelphia for several years.

Many others had never left home, or had returned there during the lean 1930s. *(Left to right)* Clarinetist "Big Eye Louis" Nelson; bass player Pops Foster; drummer Paul Barbarin; Bechet; bass player Albert Gleny; clarinetist Alphonse Picou—in New Orleans in 1944.

San Jacintos Dance Hall. Next stops: Boston and New York.

An early-'40s portrait of William Geary Johnson, of New Iberia, Louisiana. After beginning to play again, but just before coming North, Bunk and the group of somewhat younger men that had been organized to work with him could be heard in rugged New Orleans joints like the one shown above. The placard on the facing page announces the great event of late 1945: Bunk's New York debut.

212

The date is September 28, 1945, the place is Stuyvesant Casino. The lineup *(left to right):* Jim Robinson, Alcide "Slow Drag" Pavageau, Bunk, Baby Dodds, George Lewis, Alton Purnell, Lawrence Marrero. It was New York's introduction to the legendary sound of New Orleans in living form. Bunk was about sixty-six, but he had been back in practice for fully three years, and was in impressive form.

Jim Robinson's trombone was the most deep-down sound the town had heard in years.

The following year, the New Orleans Band was back at Stuyvesant. There were a few changes: Don Ewell on piano; Kaiser Marshall, once of Fletcher Henderson's orchestra, on drums; and most of the musicians were wearing jackets.

214

Bunk claimed to have been Louis Armstrong's "teacher," which stirred up considerable debate. Louis was first said to have confirmed the story, later offered a mild denial: he had listened, as a youth, in places where Bunk played, but Joe Oliver had been his principal inspiration.

One of the last pictures of this amazingly vivid, zestful, and un-docile figure from the past. It was taken in New Orleans, in 1949, the year he died.

George Lewis and the others had returned to New Orleans for a while, back to the old ways of struggling for a living by playing jazz. But the seeds had been sown: there was a growing new audience for their music in the Midwest, on the West Coast, in the East; in some clubs, at concerts, on college campuses. Lewis' 1954 band included old colleagues Purnell, Pavageau, Marrero, Robinson, plus drummer Joe Watkins and Kid Howard on trumpet. It toured most successfully for several years both here and abroad—the inset shot of Lewis in action was taken in Hamburg.

Edward "Kid" Ory had been a big man in New Orleans; in Chicago he had been a key member of Armstrong's Hot Five and Morton's Red Hot Peppers. In California, in the '30s, he was in "retirement"; but when he re-emerged in 1943 (his first appearance was on an Orson Welles radio show), he soon re-established himself as a major personage of jazz. He worked and recorded steadily, for nearly two decades thereafter, appearing in clubs and at festivals, touring Europe in the late '50s, and in general seeming much more like a top-flight tailgate trombonist than like a man born in 1886. His 1948 lineup was *(left to right)* Mutt Carey, Joe Darensbourg, Minor Hall, Ory, Bud Scott, Ed Garland; plus pianist Buster Wilson (not shown).

Henry "Red" Allen, born across the river from
New Orleans in 1908, could not be "rediscovered"—because he had never been lost or
inactive (see, for example, page 185). But the
traditionalist revival enabled him to be heard
in the good old context, as on this record session with Kid Ory.

Thomas "Papa Mutt" Carey had, like Ory,
been a Storyville jazzman; like Bunk Johnson
he had not gone up to Chicago, hence had not
recorded and was little known until the resurgence of the 1940s. He, too, provided an
exciting taste, before his death in 1948, of
what it must have been like in the good old
days. Carey played for the most part with
the Ory band, but also led groups of his own.

The resurgence of earlier jazz and its players flared up in many different areas. There was Paul Barbarin *(left)*, who had spent several years in New York with Luis Russell's big band, then returned to New Orleans in the '30s. In the late '40s he came forth again as leader of still another successful traditional-jazz group.

Lee Collins, who had recorded in New Orleans in the '20s, was active again in Chicago in the early 1950s.

Riverboat veterans like bassist Single-ton Palmer and trumpeter Dewey Jackson, of St. Louis, re-encountered long-absent success with their Dixieland Six.

Although never officially "rediscovered," the pioneers of white New Orleans jazz continued to play, largely in their home town, well into the 1950s. *Above:* Tom Brown *(left)*, the first "jass" man (see page 22), and "Papa" Jack Laine in 1952. *Directly left:* Sharkey Bonano.

For the Negro veteran, after the tumult and travel stopped for many of them, there was at least much more local playing opportunity, and places to play in, like Preservation Hall and Dixieland Hall. At the latter, in 1965: Kid Howard *(left),* and clarinetist Louis Cottrell.

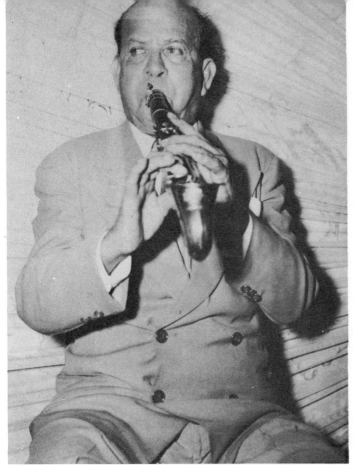

Alphonse Picou, playing an old-style French clarinet, in the early 1950s.

"Papa" Oscar Celestin (*above*) and "Kid Shots" Madison (*right*) in 1946. Celestin's Tuxedo Band remained quite active in New Orleans until his death in 1955.

Punch Miller, Chicago veteran, still playing, in New Orleans, in 1966.

The odd, but not at all incongruous, juxtaposition of Louis Armstrong's first trumpet and the curbstone from Lulu White's Mahogany Hall on this page is a fitting closing for this chapter. (The photographer, incidentally, placed the trumpet there.) For the setting is the garden of the "New Orleans Jazz Museum," and without the recent musical activity noted in the chapter it is most doubtful that there would *be* such a museum. After Bunk Johnson and the others, and the world-wide atten-

tion paid to them, it must have been a lot easier for the dedicated enthusiasts to get their fellow citizens to take this particular local cultural heritage more seriously. The "rediscovered" old-timers of jazz accomplished several things (including sparking the interest of younger musicians, as noted in the next chapter): above all, they admirably displayed traditional jazz for the very first time, to a number of people, as a vital and truly *living* force.

18

Emperor Norton's Hunch

THE WAY Lu Watters and the others saw it, you had to go back to the grass-roots New Orleans style and sound, even in San Francisco in 1940. To them it was quite clear that jazz had accumulated a good deal of dead wood and had taken more than one wrong turn in the road in the past decade and a half. To them the only thing to do was to turn back the clock and make their own fresh start. Watters was the original driving force and organizer. He formed his ideas while playing in a variety of non-jazz and semi-jazz bands that literally and figuratively took him far afield (one job was on a boat that took him as far as China). He listened to records and took part in after-hours sessions and gradually found musicians who thought, or were ready to think, as he did. By 1940 he had gathered around him the Yerba Buena Jazz Band; they had found a club in which to settle down and, with rather surprising speed, developed a faithful following. The traditionalist, or neo-classic, jazz revival was under way.

Their underlying concepts were unique in jazz, although the process of deliberately using the work of old masters as the starting point for new creative activity is by no means unknown in other fields. To these men, the music they heard around them and the bands with which they had played—they were all experienced professionals—offered strong evidence in support of their feeling that the last fully satisfactory jazz group had been King Oliver's Creole Jazz Band. (They also had a deep affection for the work of Jelly Roll Morton, but his most impressive accomplishments had been with combinations formed solely for recording purposes, leaving Oliver as the best possible all-round foundation stone.) Thus they undertook to disregard all of Swing, all big-band jazz, and all previous white variations on the New Orleans style. They absorbed their music from Oliver and Morton, from ragtime and the brass bands. They studied source material in unusually thorough fashion—early recordings, early published music, early musicians with whom they both consulted and played. They were also influenced, in part knowingly but perhaps more deeply than they realized, by the whole California tradition of "good time music" that had existed since Barbary Coast days.

What they were doing was daring in several respects: to turn back, to claim (contrary to standard theory) that a jazz form could be re-created far outside the context of time and place in which it had been born; to seek deliberately to be influenced. There was danger their music would be stale, self-conscious, even note-for-note imitation. Their most extreme detractors have claimed it did turn out pretty much that way. But to a great many others, it was quite the opposite: a vivid, fresh extension of traditional forms that had nothing even remotely academic about it and that—largely through the impact of the several strong personalities in the band—added a distinctive flavor all its own.

They became a latter-day legend, and for a while they played in splendid musical isolation. Then for a time they suddenly found themselves the spearhead of a full-scale resurgence, in other parts of the country as well as on the West Coast. Not all the new bands were of the best; few stayed together as units for very long. And eventually, as time went by and it got to be two decades and more since 1940, the remaining Yerba Buenans were more like veterans than young revolutionaries. But their own performances, and those of at least some of their disciples, had done much to prove that the early jazz was a continuing, living force, that it remained music still worth *playing*. They may not really have founded a musical empire, but they did come a lot closer to *their* goal than that mad "Emperor" Norton of the preceding century, who for no good reason at all believed himself to be the ruler of San Francisco.

Lu Watters (center) and some Yerba Buena colleagues.

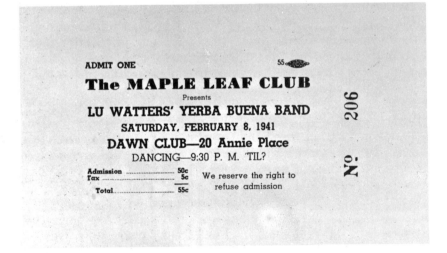

Grand Opening

HAMBONE KELLY'S

204 San Pablo Ave. • El Cerrito

FRIDAY, JUNE 20

LU WATTERS'
YERBA BUENA JAZZ BAND

• Restaurant and Bar Opens at 5:00 P.M. Daily
Except Mondays • Private Banquet Room for
Club Parties • Good Food Served Family
Style or A La Carte • A Jazz Band Plays
Every Friday, Saturday and Sunday Night
• 20-Minute Service on the "L" Bus from San
Francisco • No admission or Cover Charge at
Any Time • Free Parking • 350 Car Capacity

In these cards, an outline of the main steps in the history
of the Watters band: the early-1941 ticket from their
pre-war stand at the Dawn Club; the large poster an-
nouncing the band has been put together again after the
war and is back in business; finally, the June, 1947 opening at their own place, Hambone Kelly's, where they
were to remain through 1949.

224

The brass was the heart of the Yerba Buena sound. In the upper photo, Watters is flanked by his two main disciples, Turk Murphy (left) and Bob Scobey. Below are two other highly talented charter band-members, clar- inetist Helm and pianist Rose. (The others in the full-group picture on page 222 are Dick Lammi, tuba; Harry Mordecai, banjo; Bill Dart, drums.)

Bob Helm.

Wally Rose.

225

Various differences, including Lu Watters' own nonconformist ways, managed to split apart the "classic" band by 1951. Turk Murphy became a bandleader and has remained one. This 1952 group, at San Francisco's Italian Village, had Bob Helm and Wally Rose, Dick Lammi (now on banjo); and Bob Short on tuba. In the mid-'60s, Turk resided at his own club, "Earthquake McGoon's," in the same city, with Bob Helm still with him (*that* association having weathered many road trips and personnel changes).

Trumpeter Bob Scobey also led his own groups, usually Chicago-based, until his death in the early '60s. But Scobey preferred a looser style than that of Watters, and more "swing" to the music than a two-beat rhythm section can provide. His 1955 band, shown here, included flexible Dick Lammi (now a bassist), trombonist Jack Buck, Bill Napier on clarinet, and featured the warm vocalizing of banjoist Clancy Hayes.

The traditionalist "revival" produced several notable piano men, all of whom happened to be accomplished ragtimers: Burt Bales *(above, left)*; Paul Lingle *(above, center)*, who later emigrated to Hawaii; Don Ewell *(above, right)*, best known for his stint with Bunk Johnson; and Dick Wellstood, the only non-West Coaster, and most influenced by the Harlem stride pianists.

Young clarinetist Bob Wilber had studied with Bechet and led a high-school group in New York that included Wellstood. This 1950 group typifies the East Coast mixing of old and young; the lineup has Pops Foster on bass, trombonist Jimmy Archey, and Wellstood.

The first important followers of the Yerba Buena creed on the West Coast—banjoist Monte Ballou's Castle Jazz Band, of Portland, Oregon. This late-'40s line-up includes Bob Short on tuba, Don Kinch on trumpet, trombonist George Bruns (more famous as composer of a 1955 top song hit about Davy Crockett).

The somewhat incredible Firehouse Five Plus Two, led by trombonist Ward Kimball, are collectors of old fire engines and railroad cars, were taken up as a fad by Hollywood (most of them are Walt Disney artists). It's hard to define the relative proportions of jazz and corn in their output, but they are an unquestionably spirited outfit, always great fun to hear.

The Dixieland Rhythm Kings, originally of Dayton, Ohio, led by tuba player Gene Mayl, featuring trombonist Charlie Sonnanstine, in 1955.

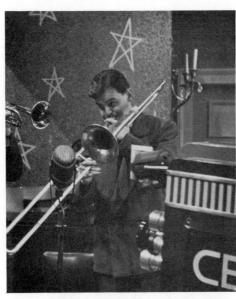

Conrad Janis attracted much attention in New York in the '50s by doubling as actor and bandleader.

Trumpeter Frank Assunto's Dukes of Dixieland, who were from New Orleans.

As has been noted, Lu Watters' colleagues did *not* build an empire, but on the whole their efforts were (as someone once said) both educational and amusing. "Educational" because it is always important to explore the past and to prove its continuing validity: and this is what was done, in one way, by the rediscovery of Bunk Johnson and in another (and equally important) way by the Yerba Buena band and its successors. "Amusing" because everybody almost always had a good time, players *and* listeners, which is no small accomplishment. And if in more than a few instances their followers turned out to be either deliberately cornball or deliberately commercial, or with more enthusiasm than ability, that's too bad, but should not detract from our appreciation of the pioneers of 1940.

19

Groovin' High

THE WAY Dizzie Gillespie and Charlie Parker and the others saw it, you had to find new changes, new chord progressions, new pathways. Starting namelessly at a long series of informal experimental sessions, their new music finally burst upon the world in the early '40s under such names as "re-bop," "be-bop," and finally just "bop," phrases supposedly suggested by the sound of the music. Whatever else it was or wasn't, it most decidedly produced a total upheaval in jazz.

The development of bop took place almost entirely at a small Harlem club called Minton's Playhouse—which surely makes it different to begin with, certainly the only time a specific address can be provided for the origins of a new jazz style. Obviously this does not mean that the style sprang into being overnight there, nor that no one had a new idea in this idiom before or outside of Minton's. But the club was a musicians' hangout, its small bandstand always open to those who wanted to sit in. And when Teddy Hill, a former swing-band leader, became its manager early in 1941, the "modern" sound really began to take over. The first band that Hill hired included Thelonious Monk and Kenny Clarke, who were already beginning to think in terms of new approaches to piano and drums, respectively, and who were to be important pioneers of bop. There were several others consistently on hand, most prominently Dizzy Gillespie, Charlie Parker (who that year had come to New York for the first time, with the Jay McShann band), Charlie Christian (who lugged his guitar and amplifier uptown after his night's work with Benny Goodman). Together and in varying combinations they began working out the new harmonic and rhythmic variations.

Gillespie was in the forefront when the music made its first big splash on 52nd Street during World War II, and he remained the public symbol of bop, in addition to being an overpowering influence on virtually all its trumpet men (as Parker was on saxophone players). The first success appears to have stirred up, among other things, an unduly large crop of writers, both friendly and unfriendly, probing into its deeper significances and theorizing as to the "why" of it all. It seems clear that it stemmed in part from a dissatisfaction with big-band Swing, which these men found stagnant and constricting. And it was also described as a music of Negro social protest (the sincere conversion of several boppers to Mohammedanism was linked with this); and it was damned as "musical anarchy" and raucous exhibitionism. Its emphasis on musical complexity was seen variously as an awareness of European serious music and as a deliberate spurning of traditional jazz. To its most ardent supporters, bop was the inevitable wave of the future. By those who were more interested in the sensational than the musical aspects (a category that included several national-circulation magazines), it was looked on as entirely a mixture of narcotics addiction, weird appearance (goatees, berets, dark glasses) and a very "hip" special slang.

Bop did have its share of dubious quirks and of inferior musicians and cultism, and some purely commercial nonsense attached itself to its fringes. Above all, this was certainly not an easily understandable music, particularly for ears accustomed to earlier jazz forms. For it was drastically, radically, even frighteningly different, with its deliberately flatted notes and dissonant chords and the like. But it is exactly this difference—and its apparently permanent impact upon the course of jazz—that gives this whole movement its claim to lasting importance.

Dizzy Gillespie.

In 1941, which came to be considered the first official year of modern jazz, the two titans of the period to come were holding down routine big-band jobs. Twenty-four-year old John Gillespie is the trumpeter at the left in the Cab Calloway band *(upper photo)*. An early "Dizzy" legend notes that he left Cab after a fight over a spitball he probably *didn't* throw. Charlie Parker, aged twenty-one, is the second from the left in the reed section of Jay McShann's blues-playing band from Kansas City, shown at the Savoy Ballroom in Harlem.

232

Earl "Father" Hines' big band now sounded quite different from the way it did in Chicago in the '30s: by 1943 it was home for both Gillespie (*far left*) and Parker (*far right*). In this picture, taken at New York's Apollo Theater in April of that year, Sarah Vaughan is the girl at the piano.

Billy Eckstine (*left*) with Charlie Parker at the 1950 opening of the night club called Birdland (a name derived from Parker's standard nickname, "Yardbird," later shortened to "Bird"). They were old friends: Eckstine was Earl Hines's vocalist in '43, was fascinated by the new sounds. His ahead-of-its-times touring band of 1944-45 marked the first significant public association of Gillespie and Parker.

Fifty-second Street remained a hectic center of musical activity throughout most of the '40s. The very first bop band there, put together by Dizzy and bassist Oscar Pettiford, played at the Onyx Club *(upper photo)* in 1944, with Don Byas on tenor sax, young Max Roach on drums, very young George Wallington on piano. In the photo below, on the same street at about the same time, veteran Coleman Hawkins led a band that included Byas, trumpeter Benny Harris (who had sat next to Dizzy in the Earl Hines band), drummer Denzil Best, and the youthful piano player who had been at Minton's—Thelonious Monk.

234

Much has been made of bop being a violent breaking away from the past, but there were key transitional figures, like Lester Young *(right)*. The sensitive man they called "Prez" (meaning "President of All the Saxophone Players") exerted vast influence on the newcomers. He worked with them *(below, right*—with Pettiford, Dizzy, Wallington)* only rarely. But for a full decade his light, dry tenor-sax sound was the ideal.

Coleman Hawkins, shown below with Gillespie, was sympathetic, proved adaptable, became deeply involved with the new music at the start; but to many boppers his "heavy" tone was out of fashion.

Pictures of Bird and Diz together are rather rare, since they went their separate ways after the mid-'40s. This happy reunion took place on a 52nd-Street bandstand in 1950 (as a taste of the future, note that the baby-faced tenorman peering in at the right is John Coltrane). Four years earlier the two had journeyed to Los Angeles, where the photos below were taken, to meet largely unsympathetic audiences and much frustration.

In early '46, Gillespie and Ross Russell (head of the bop-pioneering Dial record label), in a pose that emphasizes Dizzy's flair for playing the clown. *Above:* Parker, with be-spectacled young Erroll Garner, bassist Red Callender *(right)*, and drummer Harold West *(left)* at a 1947 record date for Dial, shortly after Bird left a California state sanitarium.

Gillespie, who was the focal point of most of the publicity about bop, was also about the only leader able to achieve even brief big-band success. He did so several times: the poster below is for a 1947 concert. In his 1948 band *(above)* could be found trumpeter Benny Harris, Al McKibbon on bass, and saxophonists Ernie Henry *(second from left)* and Yusef Lateef *(second from right)*. In the early '50s he was back in a small-band setting for a while *(below)* and with that up-tilted horn, created (according to various tales) either on purpose or by being accidentally stepped on.

Erroll Garner was *with* the modern movement rather than *of* it. Above all he is an individual stylist and a phenomenally popular one, with both jazz and non-jazz listeners. What less can be said of a man who has moved from 52nd Street and record dates with Bird to being presented as an S. Hurok attraction?

Bud Powell, brilliant and erratic, who had hung around Minton's as a teen-ager, became probably the most important influence on young pianists of the '40s and '50s, with a style in which the left hand plays a subordinate role. His technique and energy were fantastic, but a series of mental breakdowns since the late '40s have left his work largely a promise and an influence.

Thelonious Monk is generally recognized as belonging with Gillespie and Parker in a Big Three of early-modernist innovators. He was in the house band at Minton's, but acclaim was much slower in coming to him. The personal eccentricities, both real and fancied, for which he was most widely known may have been part of the problem; the very real complexity and difficulty of his music was also a factor. Above all, Monk was never a joiner; he could not be part of any "school" except his own. He has always been a paradox: criticized as a crude pianist yet composer of some of the most lyrical melodies (*'Round Midnight, Ruby My Dear*); a famous legend yet scarcely heard except by insiders until the mid-'50s. His major impact and success came after that—so his story is picked up in the next chapter.

Fats Navarro, who took over Dizzy's chair in the Eckstine band, gave promise of vast originality; but he died, of tuberculosis, in 1950. His setting here is the Royal Roost, bop's first Broadway home; his companions are Allen Eager, one of the better tenor sax players, and Kenny Clarke, one of the Minton's pioneers.

These two young horn men began their careers in this period of musical upheaval and have flourished ever since—a very long time in this business. Trombonist J. J. Johnson (left) blew into town from Indianapolis in 1943, aged 19, and remained the unquestioned, poll-winning master of his instrument ever after. St. Louis-born Miles

Davis is shown with Charlie Parker, with whom he was working and recording in the mid-'40s, when he was perhaps barely 20. Miles was quickly noticeable as a bop trumpet who did *not* sound like a carbon copy of Dizzy, and his clear, "cool" tone was to have tremendous effect on the decade to come.

Unquestionably, a major career was cut short when Clifford Brown (*above*), a trumpet player of vast power and grace, was killed in a 1956 auto accident. He had formed a most close-knit team with Max Roach (*above, right*) one of the great innovators of modern drumming. The '54 band, in the bottom photo, included Harold Land on tenor; by '56 Brownie was teamed with the up-and-coming Sonny Rollins (*center photo*).

Young Milt Jackson, first to make "vibes" (brought to prominence by hard-swinging musicians like Lionel Hampton and Red Norvo) an important part of modern jazz and an instrument of great subtlety. Later he was a charter member of the Modern Jazz Quartet.

In the work of Art Blakey *(above)*, Max Roach, and Kenny Clarke, a new concept of jazz drums was first put into practice: these men sought to make the drummer a full-fledged instrumentalist, not just the man in the background who keeps time for the others.

Oscar Pettiford *(left)* and Ray Brown *(right)*, finest of a new breed of bassist. The function of the bass player altered fully as much as that of the drummer. The emergence of this rhythm instrument as one suitable for melodic solo efforts can be traced directly to

the late Jimmy Blanton and his 1939-41 work with Duke Ellington. The leading bop bassists made no secret of the fact that they idolized Blanton and were following a trail he had blazed.

George Shearing arrived from England in the late '40s and quickly proved an exception to the rule about Europeans not making the grade in American jazz. His first (1949) quintet has John Levy on bass, vibist Margie Hyams, guitarist Chuck Wayne, and drummer Denzil Best. The unique piano-vibes blend brought swift success; the sound was a non-turbulently swinging one, but clearly derived from the new rhythmic freedom of bop.

The fame and fortune that came to Shearing (and eventually moved him away from the jazz scene) made him an exception among the several white bop pianists. Al Haig (left), Dodo Marmorosa (right), and the previously noted George Wallington were all closely involved in early modernism, but Al and Dodo merely faded from the scene into obscurity.

Don Byas was basically a swing-style tenorman (for example, he was with Count Basie in 1941) but with some advanced ideas. He worked briefly with Gillespie, but since 1946 has remained in Europe, making him the forerunner of a steady stream of modernist expatriate musicians. (Yes, that's Erroll Garner on piano in the background.)

Dexter Gordon (*left*) and Lucky Thompson (*above*) stood out among the tenor men of the period. Gordon was part of the Billy Eckstine band, so was Thompson, whose clear tone seems (rarity of rarities) not exactly in either the Hawkins or the Young "school" of tenor sax.

Impresario Norman Grantz, whose "Jazz at the Philharmonic" concert tours provided much employment and exposure for jazzmen in the late '40s and '50s, did things in a big way, mixing ex-Swing, ex-Ellington, modern and what-not in large doses. Such as *(above, left to right)* Johnny Hodges, Flip Phillips, Lionel Hampton, Illinois Jacquet, Oscar Peterson, Buddy Rich and Ray Brown *(rear)*, and Dizzy Gillespie. JATP was also a home for Charlie Parker at times: the studio scene *(left)* indicates that Benny Carter, Bird, Phillips and Ben Webster were all recording for Grantz simultaneously!

There was also a big-band sound abroad in the land, known at times as "progressive" jazz, making use of the ideas of modern European composers, sometimes highly exciting and at other times pretentious. Above all, it was California-based Stan Kenton's music. Always a most serious craftsman and experimenter, Kenton's efforts and effects have been controversial, but his sincerity and drive were never questioned. *Above:* in the recording studio; arranger Pete Rugolo is at the far left. *Below:* his 1951 band, including, at Kenton's right, saxophonists Art Pepper *(left)* and Bud Shank, and, behind some of those trumpet bells, men like Shorty Rogers and Maynard Ferguson. The left-hand photo shows Kenton and part of his 1944 sax section, including one of the major stylists of the period ahead: Stan Getz *(left)*.

Despite tight-knit ensemble arrangements and the perfectionist drive of its leader, the various editions of the Kenton band produced several noted individual stars. Some are noted on the facing page; herewith some others:

Actually, a whole new "school" of jazz singing came into being: Anita O'Day (*above*) could be said to have created it (1944-5) as an offshoot of her 1941-3 style with Gene Krupa's band; and June Christy (*left*) certainly brought it to perfection during the late '40s.

Kai Winding (*above*), born in Denmark, toured with Kenton in '47, went on to work with the Eastern boppers and won much jazz acclaim for his mid-'50s trombone pairing with J. J. Johnson. Drummer Shelly Manne used different geography: New York-born, after several stints with Kenton (and one with Woody Herman) he left the East to become a permanent Californian.

Boyd Raeburn's band was in existence for only a few years, beginning in 1944, but its jazz output could compare favorably with any band of its day. Much of the credit went to arranger George Handy *(left)*, who had studied with Aaron Copland. The band perished from a common jazz ailment: lack of commercial success.

Claude Thornhill did not exactly have a jazz band in '46 and thereafter, but he created rich and richly admired sounds with the aid of key arrangers like Gil Evans and (later) Gerry Mulligan.

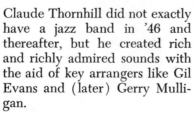

Woody Herman's "First Herd" seemed to find itself suddenly: for some time there had been gradual replacement of drafted members of Woody's blues-playing band, but no startlingly "modern" sounds until their first Columbia record session, pictured below, in February, 1945. The upper photo displays the impressive trumpet section of (left to right) Sonny Berman, Neal Hefti, Ray Linn, brothers Pete and Conte Condoli. Bill Harris is the middle trombonist; the drummer is Dave Tough, the ever-expanding Chicagoan who bridged so many styles so well. In the lower photo the other rhythm men are pianist Ralph Burns, guitarist Billy Bauer, Chubby Jackson on bass. At the left of the sax section is "Flip" Phillips, with John La Porta next to him.

Some stars of the Herds: Bill Harris *(left)*; Flip Phillips *(center)*; Sonny Berman, who flared brightly, died young.

Serge Chaloff, baritone sax, of the Second Herd.

Two original Herdsmen, Berman *(left)* and Chubby Jackson *(right)*, flank two additions: trumpeter Shorty Rogers and drummer Don Lamond, who continued as key members when Woody re-organized in 1947. . . . And then he re-organized many times over, one of the few to keep a band alive through the years, charging into the 1960s with everything changing except Woody Herman's own enthusiasm and vigor.

Sarah Vaughan, like Ella Fitzgerald before her, won an amateur competition at Harlem's Apollo Theater, and took off from there. Billy Eckstine heard her in 1942, and recommended her to Earl Hines. In '44 she was with Eckstine's band, and in most of her singing for a long time thereafter the influence of the modern musicians she worked with was apparent in the graceful bending of notes ("as if she were an instrument") that became her special trademark.

Jackie (Cain) and Roy (Kral), a unique husband-and-wife team whose highly effective, bop-influenced unison vocals were featured with the late-'40s bands of tenorman Charlie Ventura (right).

New faces came onto the scene, began to grow toward stardom which would long outlast "bop." Horace Silver, brilliant young Bud Powell-influenced pianist, left an Art Blakey group in 1956 to form his first band *(above)*, with Doug Watkins, bass; Hank Mobley on tenor sax; Art Farmer, trumpet.

Young men with post-bop futures: Hank Mobley and trumpeter Donald Byrd had been with Silver in Blakey's 1955 "Jazz Messengers."

In the fast-changing world of jazz, constancy can be a comfort. Hefty-toned sax men Sonny Stitt *(left)* and Gene Ammons were a "battle of the tenors" team in 1950—and again in the '60s.

The early-1949 recording session featuring the *Metronome* poll winners—for a significant contrast see the pictures on page 183. With the single exception of Dixielander Ernie Caceres, the personnel is strictly modernist.

(Standing next to guitarist Bauer is Pete Rugolo, the year's award-winning arranger. Shelly Manne is the drummer.)

Two signs of the times: above is the neon that proclaimed "Bop City" at the turn of the '50s. It was an ambitious night spot, and as short-lived as most. Birdland, however, did much better with a similar policy (modern jazz, an admission charge, and a "bullpen" for those who wanted only to listen, not drink). Its life-span was, for a club, quite amazing: 1950-1965.

The hard, heavy early outbursts of bop were giving way to various other things, with "cool" as the key word. These photos underline the transition. *Above:* the Modern Jazz Quartet was formed in 1952. In '55, drummer Kenny Clarke was replaced by Connie Kay; and Milt Jackson *(left)*, pianist-composer-musical director John Lewis, and Percy Heath *(right)* were ready for things to come. *Left* is Miles Davis, who was to influence the '50s much as Diz and Bird had the '40s; at the piano is arranger-composer Tadd Dameron, who from the start had stressed the "prettier" side of the bop world.

"Be-bop" was above all an impact; it became a feverish fad, and a combination of its own weaknesses and the way in which it was exploited brought about its end, as a self-contained style, in relatively short order. But the effects of the revolution clearly will never die down; many ex-boppers, and many other musicians influenced by them, continued to create "new" jazz of varying types and quality in the decades that followed. Charlie Parker, co-founder of bop, and one who seemed most unlikely to let his music stop changing and become stagnant, can bring the chapter to a neatly symbolic close. "Bird" was ill and rather out of favor in some musical circles in the early '50s, yet it now seems clear that he must be considered the true genius of early modern jazz. The man died in March, 1955; a decade and more later, his influence is still heard, undiminished, in the sound of a vast number of musicians and bands.

20

Now's the Time

A GREAT MANY fascinating things always seem to be happening—or just about to happen—or perhaps to have just come to an end. And, largely as a result of all this ferment and activity, but also because it is difficult to count and classify the trees when you are standing in the middle of the forest, there is an almost total absence of perspective.

It is difficult enough to estimate what will seem to have been the significant elements of the current jazz scene when the time comes to look back at it from the vantage point of next week (*any* next week). It seems quite impossible to guess at long-range values, to separate the wheat from the chaff in most cases with any feeling of certainty, to "know" what paths will ultimately turn out to be the fruitful ones, which decisions will prove to have been the right ones, or which musicians will eventually be judged the major figures.

Since jazz remains a living, breathing, ever-changing music, it is obvious that all books about jazz should be so constructed that they can be left open at the end. This being physically unfeasible, the alternative is that this concluding chapter be different in character from any that came before it. Instead of depicting the faces and settings that make up, more or less, a unity of time or style, or tell the story of a single significant man, this must be a montage. (And since this is a revised edition of this book, it is embarrassingly easy to remember how quickly and devastatingly the passage of time robbed the original last chapter of its pretensions to prophecy, its validity, even its common sense.)

Here, then, are many of the people who make up the jazz scene of today, of the few years of the most immediate past, and (hopefully) of the next few years. It is a selection—more of a sampling than a total picture. And of course it need not be concerned with things already brought up to date in preceding chapters: the continuing sagas of Armstrong and Ellington, the status of Dixieland and the traditional New Orleans style, and of the blues.

What it does accomplish is a survey of trends and of the many individual stars, established and new, tracing a somewhat chronological path through the rise and fall of post-bop West Coast coolness and Eastern "hard bop" (or neo-bop, or what-you-will), through soul music and bossa nova and other phenomena, on to the "new thing" revolution. And much more. Much of the period, though obviously not all, bears the mark of Miles Davis and various of his talented ex-sidemen, which is one reason why he is looking over this page. (Although, to be precise, he is looking *away* from it, which is appropriate enough, since among the things Miles became famous for were literally turning his back on audiences and leaving the bandstand during other band-members' solos.)

This would probably be a difficult period to analyze even with perspective, containing as it does so many different and conflicting elements: high spots and low ebbs for all types of jazz; the growth of the Newport Jazz Festival into a respectable, nationally known event, and the closing of so many clubs (including Birdland); major commercial success for some performers and nothing at all for others. Confusing—yes; but it is "now," and as we began by noting, it is and was and is about to be most fascinating.

Miles Davis

Dave Brubeck *(below)* was in the forefront of the early-1950s West Coast "cool" swing of the jazz pendulum. His quartet featured the alto sax of Paul Desmond *(left)*, a most consistent winner of critics' polls. The group was the most successful of that day: best-selling records, world travel, the leader's picture on a *Time* cover, etc. And, despite many changes in public taste, things have continued that way for Brubeck into the '60s. The current group includes drummer Joe Morello, bassist Gene Wright.

Gerry Mulligan

Chet Baker, Gerry Mulligan, and bassist Carson Smith

Gerry Mulligan came out of the East to form, in 1952, a most celebrated and "typically West Coast" pianoless quartet. It featured Chet Baker *(above)*, who carried a Miles Davis-type trumpet sound to extremes of great beauty (at times) and blandness (at others). Mulligan went on to a decade and more of eclecticism: organizing various small and large bands, recording with a truly staggering variety of musicians—from, say, Stan Getz *(at the left)* to Thelonious Monk (page 263).

Chico Hamilton *(below, left)* had been on drums in the 1952 Mulligan band. By 1956 he was a great success on his own, with this unusual and subtle-sounding lineup: Buddy Collette, tenor (also flute); Jim Hall, guitar; Fred Katz, cello; Carson Smith, bass. Like all bands, Chico's went through many changes of personnel and status; he might even turn out to be best remembered for giving early encouragement to avant-garde innovator Eric Dolphy, shown *(below, right)* with cellist Nathan Gershman.

In 1957, pianist Andre Previn *(above)*, one-time precocious teen-age movie arranger, recorded the score of the Broadway hit *My Fair Lady*. Among the major successes of our time, the album launched an avalanche of "jazz version of . . ." items. One-time Kenton drummer Shelly Manne *(above, right)* shared billing with Previn on that block-buster record, was also noted in the late '50s and early '60s as a Hollywood jazz-club owner, small-band leader, and remained (incidentally) a superb drummer. Guitarist Barney Kessel *(right)* was another top name of this period of Los Angeles activity; bassist Howard Ramsey's The Lighthouse *(below)*, at nearby Hermosa Beach, had featured such local jazzmen since 1948. But by the mid-'60s the tide of public attention had shifted yet again, leaving most West Coast attractions feeling dry and neglected.

Experimentation, both new and of long standing, continued on both coasts. Clarinetist Jimmy Giuffre *(left)* tried many styles and combinations, including this trio with guitarist Jim Hall and valve trombone Bobby Brookmeyer. Nonconformist, pianist, and teacher, Lennie Tristano *(below)* stays East, often associated throughout two decades with alto Lee Konitz *(below, left)*.

Tenor sax Bob Cooper *(left)*, altoist Bud Shank *(right)*, and elder statesman Shorty Rogers. Such men have often evoked a sort of post-graduate Kenton sound.

Very possibly the greatest continuing experimenter of them all is pianist Thelonious Monk, the intense and intricate Minton's veteran who wasn't widely accepted until the late '50s. Perhaps no one was ready for him at the start, but it is also true that he made few club appearances until 1957, when he first held court at New York's Five Spot Café *(top)* with the classic quartet that had John Coltrane on tenor, drummer Shadow Wilson, and bassist Wilbur Ware (not shown). Monk has recorded in varied contexts, from big orchestra to solo, including one LP with the ubiquitous Gerry Mulligan, who listens with him to a playback in the photo just above.

A musical unit that remains together for a full decade is apt to be either flawlessly meshed, a bit stagnant—or perhaps both. But the Modern Jazz Quartet, though it may swing a bit gently for some tastes, really shows no signs of stagnation. Sparked by the superior writing and taut musical direction of pianist John Lewis, they've played with success and distinction just about everywhere, including Japan *(below, left)*.

Left to right: Percy Heath, Connie Kay, John Lewis, Milt Jackson. As the formal group portrait *(below, right)* might suggest, they work more in concert halls than clubs.

An action portrait of John Lewis *(above)*. Apart from the MJQ, Lewis has been involved, with composer Gunther Schuller *(below)*, in the experimental "Orchestra USA." When "Bags" (as Jackson is known to jazzmen) works on his own, it's more apt to be on a funky, shirt-sleeves record date *(left)*.

By the late '50s the tide of jazz momentum (which is also something like a ping-pong ball) had begun to return eastward. One major reason: the full emergence of Miles Davis. He sounded as "cool" and suave as anyone out West (and had a way of playing a ballad so it broke your heart). But his soloists had more depth, and the rhythm section had vastly more fire. John Coltrane with Miles *(left)* in '58 was developing his "sheets of sound" concept, and Davis himself was delving into limpid "modal" music and perfecting his art of audience-ignoring. Then there were some startling big-band records impressively arranged by Gil Evans *(below, left)*, culminating in a 1961 Carnegie Hall concert *(below)*.

It was extremely all-star: *(left)* Miles on the stand in '56, backed by a favorite drummer, Philly Joe Jones; and *(below)* Cannonball Adderley and Bill Evans, key 1958 sidemen, at a record date.

This long-time Davis rhythm section finally went out on its own as the Wynton Kelly *(above)* Trio, with bassist Paul Chambers and drummer Jimmy Cobb.

Bill Evans did not really come to the attention of the jazz public until 1958, which was the year he spent with Miles Davis. Thereafter Evans led his own trio and swiftly rose to recognition as *the* major new creative force in jazz piano: introspective yet lyrical; thoughtful but never unswinging; and also a sensitive composer *(below)*. His position in the photo at the right, incidentally, is somewhat *less* bent than is customary. The two bottom pictures offer Evans with some interesting co-workers. Under the "Exit" sign in the rear of New York's Village Vanguard he is with his long-time trio members, drummer Paul Motian *(right)* and the highly promising bassist Scott LaFaro, just weeks before LaFaro's death in an auto accident in 1961. Doing some last-minute checking at a 1962 record date, he is flanked by guitarist Jim Hall *(left)* and drummer Philly Joe Jones.

In 1959, after leaving Miles Davis, Julian "Cannonball" Adderley *(right)* organized his own quintet, with his brother Nat on cornet, bassist Sam Jones, and drummer Lou Hayes (as *above*). At San Francisco's Jazz Workshop they recorded an album for the Riverside label, including a funky tune by pianist Bobby Timmons, *This Here*. It was as if a dam had burst, flooding the jazz scene with what was variously called "soul jazz," "church blues," or just plain "soul." It brought Cannonball and his band swift but lasting success, with their joyfully earthy brand of blues and neo-bop in the sudden forefront of a brand-new fad.

Bobby Timmons *(left)* went off on his own very shortly; their mid-'60s pianist was Austrian-born Joe Zawinul, shown *(above)* with Cannonball. Right: Nat Adderley at a rehearsal hall.

The "Jay and Kai" (Winding) team onstage with Dizzy Gillespie and his "up" horn, in 1955.

J. J. Johnson has been in and around the New York jazz scene since 1943, and almost from the start he has been *the* unquestioned master among trombonists. It is a record of both length and strength of jazz pre-eminence that is completely unmatched.

Johnson's most customary setting: a small band. This 1959 unit included tenor Clifford Jordan, drummer Al Heath.

Stan Getz, whom we noted with Kenton in '44, made his first real mark with the Woody Herman band at the end of the 1940s, and for most of the next decade his cool, Lester Young-derived sound dominated the tenor-sax scene. But once again that matter of shifting tides . . . by 1958 he was a semipermanent resident of Copenhagen, where he is shown *(below, left)* with an unidentified beer-drinker at the Café Montmartre. In 1962 he made an album with guitarist Charlie Byrd *(below):* the Getz sound and the Brazilian samba rhythm called "bossa nova" turned out to be an incredibly compatible combination, a major popular fad was launched, and Getz was back at the top of the heap.

Antonio Carlos Jobim, no jazzman, but a founding father of bossa nova; he wrote *One Note Samba* and *Desafinado,* has recorded with Getz.

Bossa nova and flutist Herbie Mann *(left)* did a lot for each other, too. Inventive and adaptable, he had scored with a group in an "Afro-Cuban" vein, but in '63 traveled as far as Rio to record *(below)* the new beat on its home grounds.

The mixture of "Afro" and Latin elements with jazz has always had strong appeal, as played by such as vibist Cal Tjader and his former sideman, conga drummer Mongo Santamaria. (Mongo added a rhythm-and-blues touch in his '63 hit, *Watermelon Man.*)

Piano-led trios have consistently reached high popularity levels. Ahmad Jamal *(left)*, whose widely spaced piano style was praised by Miles Davis, spurted to fame in '58, but then subsided. Canadian-born Oscar Peterson *(above)*, teamed with the great bassist Ray Brown (plus either guitar or drums) from 1951 through 1965, and they made believers out of just about all listeners, public and musicians alike.

Ramsey Lewis (with drummer Red Holt and bassist Eldee Young) did the near-impossible in 1965, when two of his recordings climbed to the top of the *pop* best-seller lists.

Billy Taylor (shown at the Hickory House with Earl May, bass; Percy Brice, drums, in '55) is now equally active as a disc jockey, jazz authority, commentator, etc.

A

B

C

A Sort of Jazz Family Tree, suggesting just how shifting and interlocked are the destinies of some Easterners, is on these two pages. It starts with Horace Silver *(A)* and Art Blakey *(F)* who led the mid-'50s Jazz Messengers, which included Donald Byrd *(C)*. Horace's own first group had Art Farmer *(B)*, although throughout the early '60s he worked with the team of Blue Mitchell, trumpet, and Junior Cook, tenor *(D)*. Blakey used Lee Morgan *(G)*, tenorman-arranger Benny Golson (in *E*) and pianist Bobby Timmons *(H)*, perhaps Silver's closest rival as a blues composer. In '58, Golson-and-Farmer *(E)* formed their "Jazztet," which also included Curtis Fuller *(I)*. But by the early '60s, Fuller had joined a new Messengers lineup along with tenor Wayne Shorter and trumpet Freddie Hubbard *(J)*. Any questions? Oh, yes, for the most part it all sounded pretty funky on blues tunes, and "hard bop" on the up-tempo numbers.

E

F

G

H

J

I

Except for Art Blakey, Max Roach *(left)* was the only post-bop drummer to operate consistently as a working band-leader. After the death of Clifford Brown in 1956, Roach's quintet featured trumpeter Kenny Dorham—one of the best and most underrated—along with Sonny Rollins *(below)*. Later, a wide variety of promising young artists passed through his band and were subjected to his musical influence. For example, in 1958, there was a tuba player: Ray Draper, who is visible in the photo on the left.

Just as Kenny Clarke, Roach, and Blakey had been revolutionary influences on the young drummers of the '40s, so was Philly Joe Jones *the* drummer of the middle and late 1950s. His position with Miles Davis brought attention, and his fiery, showboat performances were widely copied. Actually, he was a bad influence on those drummers unable to grasp the subtly shaded end of his broad range of dynamics. Much the same was true of the next "in" drummer, the unrelated Elvin Jones *(right)*, who built percussive patterns of great intricacy and force with John Coltrane that were not easy for young drummers of the '60s either to understand or to emulate.

A rare early glimpse, probably from around 1950, of a young and startlingly long-haired Sonny Rollins.

Rollins, with two drummers (Billy Higgins and Mickey Roker) and beret, plays in the rain at a 1964 concert in the garden of New York's Museum of Modern Art.

Obviously one of the major saxophone stylists of modern jazz—more accurately, *two* of them—Sonny Rollins is no easy man to describe. After leaving Max Roach in '57, he leaped to a commanding position: the top tenorman of the hard-bop school, restoring to favor the deep and heavy Coleman Hawkins-style sound. Suddenly, in 1959, he left the scene for two years of soul-searching, and returned with a vastly different conception, aggressively attuned to the new "freedom" of the jazz of the '60s. *Above*, he stands tall and impressive as he plays at a Newport Jazz Festival. At the *right*, with Coleman Hawkins—both a suggestion of their musical kinship and a reminder of the near-immortality of the fabulous Hawk, who was the very first top man among tenor players.

For some five years after 1958, this group epitomized real *jazz* singing—uniquely offering the lyrics Jon Hendricks *(right)* had put to instrumental choruses. At their self-created vocal craft, (Dave) Lambert, Hendricks and (Annie) Ross were incomparable.

From 1954 into the '60s, Joe Williams *(left)* just about revived the art of big-band singing, as he hollered blues and sang ballads for Count Basie. Ray Charles *(below)* is admittedly a rhythm-and-blues singer, but he is also, by universal agreement, a "genius" who transcends boundary lines and must be accepted as part of jazz.

There is very little to be said about these ladies except the one-word poem: "Listen!" Ella Fitzgerald *(left)* remains the moving artist she has always been, only perhaps more so. Carmen McRae *(below, left,* with arranger Ernie Wilkins) has developed into one of the most effective stylists of the '60s. Dinah Washington *(below, right)* was, like Ray Charles, a bridge between the worlds of blues, pop, and jazz. Her death in 1963 left a gap that will not be filled.

The organ, once listed in jazz polls as "miscellaneous instrument," is no longer that way at all. Not in the hands of the current crop of hard-driving, earthy pounders, most notably Jimmy Smith *(left)*, one of the strongest sellers of the middle '60s. On some records his hefty sound was even further enhanced by big-band scores. *Below:* Smith with arranger Oliver Nelson.

Shirley Scott *(above)* is one of several organists who have met with much acceptance from a club audience all across the country that goes for a basic beat. Vibes player Johnny Lytle *(right)*, a favorite on that same club circuit, works with a trio that includes an organ.

The '50s and '60s abounded in highly skilled pianists, some more or less buried in bands or studio work, some featured with trios of their own; playing in a variety of styles. This is, of necessity, an arbitrary and incomplete page-and-a-half sampling. But it does begin properly, with Wynton Kelly *(right)*, considered by many horn men as the almost perfect supporting hands. *Below:* a pensive view of Barry Harris, talented upholder of the Tatum tradition. *Middle:* Hank Jones; warm, fluent, rarely able to get out of the broadcasting and recording studios.

Above: Randy Weston, lyrical, a fine composer, and six-and-a-half feet tall. *Far left:* Phineas Newborn, a brilliant talent, held back by mental illness. *Left:* Don Friedman, an experimenter toward new things; the bassist is Chuck Israels (part of Bill Evans' trio since 1961).

Three of the most blues-filled pianists, starting fittingly with Junior Mance:

Middle: Les McCann, a very funky sound. *Just above:* Mose Allison, a voice as bluesy as his piano.

Until late in 1958, Wes Montgomery *(above)* was strictly a legend, a self-taught, Charlie Christian-influenced myth in Indianapolis. Then he hit New York, and most other guitarists probably wished he had stayed home. Using his thumb (no pick), Wes specializes in block chords and octave runs, which are physically "impossible" on the instrument. His playing is full of roots and blues and emotion, and he scarcely reads music—apparently "technique" is a natural part of this man, not something to be acquired.

The other guitarists of the day are far from second-raters. Jim Hall *(left)* and bossa-nova introducer Charlie Byrd *(above)* are living proof that it's possible to be technically adept and still play with fire and strength. Grant Green *(below, left)* is a formidable blues man, a driving, fundamental guitarist. Kenny Burrell *(below)* fits just about any bag with unfailing swing and taste.

On these pages, a sampling, obviously incomplete, of the formidable array of saxophone talent on hand in the post-bop '50s and '60s:

Johnny Griffin (For a time, Griff and Lockjaw Davis were an earthshaking tenor team.)

Jackie McLean

Sonny Stitt

Lou Donaldson

James Moody

Left: Eddie "Lockjaw" Davis, more than once a Basie mainstay. *Bottom left:* Yusef Lateef, master of tenor, flute, oboe. *Just below:* Just about inseparable since Woody Herman Herd days—Zoot Sims *(left)* and Al Cohn. *Bottom right:* baritone sax Pepper Adams.

This *might* be a symposium on "What Direction for Jazz?" or something, but it's actually just a fairly whimsical way of pointing up the role of the conductor-arranger in jazz today. All those shown here are serious and able folk; as composers and/or arrangers, they are often called upon to conduct recordings of their work; as conductors they use their arms in different, highly personal ways—and to us it suggested a pattern.

Thus Gil Evans (*top left*) only seems to be warding off a jab from the right by brilliant young arranger-recording executive Quincy Jones. It only seems as if (in descending order) avant-garde composer and bandleader George Russell is cajoling; hard-swinging arranger Ernie Wilkins is defensive; the late Tadd Dameron is forcefully closing in; and arranger Melba Liston is obviously confused by it all!

Men at Work: Below, three of the finest trumpet men of any era—but all went from big-band sections into the TV and recording studios, which is no way to get famous. Thus they are far less renowned than their talents warrant: Clark Terry *(top);* Thad Jones *(middle);* and Joe Wilder.

More Forgotten Men: For a bassist who doesn't hog solos the rhythm section can be pretty anonymous, too. Some bows, then, to Sam Jones and Percy Heath (in conversation with Bobby Timmons—*top*); Ron Carter, recording at the Village Vanguard (with drummer Albert Heath—*middle*); Jimmy Garrison and Art Davis, working tandem (with Elvin Jones at a John Coltrane record date).

In 1950, Charlie Mingus was slim, clean-shaven, and the only unbilled member of "The Red Norvo Trio featuring Tal Farlow." Later, his ego was more to be reckoned with.

Mingus in close-up. (Actually, he is playing the piano here.)

A forceful bassist, but more important as a bandleader, a composer who utilizes both blues roots and advanced dissonances, a restless and argumentative soul noted for telling inattentive audiences *exactly* what he thinks of them. Mingus was closely associated with the original Five Spot Café (where Monk played so often, too). At the *right,* the club's jam-packed 1963 closing-night celebration, with Mingus deep in conversation with baritone saxophonist Pepper Adams, a frequent band-member.

Every so often it seems time for revolution, or for a prophet to appear bearing a new gospel. But how many can really tell if it's a liberator or an opportunist on the horizon, a messiah or a charlatan in the pulpit? In 1959, Ornette Coleman, a one-time Texas rhythm-and-blues musician, came to New York from Los Angeles armed with a plastic alto, a new jazz, the support of John Lewis ("the only really new thing since . . . the mid-'40s") and much critical acclaim. Briefly, Coleman's music involved improvisation without dependence on previously established chord patterns. In a word: *freedom*. In another: *anarchy*. Most jazzmen scoffed initially, and Ornette himself never scored widely with the jazz public. But in the next half-dozen years a great many established musicians had adopted greater or lesser amounts of that "freedom" in their playing, and an extremely free new crop had sprung up. It may still be too soon for proper perspective on Ornette, but only a deaf man could deny that a "new thing" was on hand.

Coleman and plastic saxophone with Nesuhi Ertegun *(above)* of Atlantic, who recorded him several times. At the *right:* Coleman and close associate Don Cherry, with his pocket trumpet.

Eric Dolphy

Roland Kirk

Three more for the future book:
pianist Denny Zeitlin, also a
doctor; Charles Lloyd and guitarist Gabor Szabo.

On this page, glimpses of a few who appear involved in expanding
jazz horizons. Cecil Taylor *(above)* predates Ornette Coleman, has
been asserting his fervidly unorthodox approach to the piano since
the mid-'50s. Roland Kirk at first appears a trickster: he is blind and
plays up to three reeds at once (including a *manzella* and a *strich*),
but there is dedication rather than gimmickry in his passionate
sound. Eric Dolphy graduated from a Chico Hamilton group,
evolved a highly personal and angular style on bass clarinet, flute
and alto sax, gained considerable attention during a stint with John
Coltrane, then suddenly died during a 1964 European tour.

In the pages of this book it has been possible to watch John Coltrane develop, in some fifteen years, from a rather shy young be-bopper with Diz and Bird (page 236) to an elder statesman (next page). He would appear to have emerged from his late-'50s service with Monk and Miles with his heart and mind firmly on the future. Perhaps touched somewhat by what he heard in Ornette Coleman, he has himself exerted influence over virtually all young saxophonists (and even some older ones, who admit to wanting to "play those 'snakes' sounds like 'Trane does"). He has benefited from long and close association with pianist McCoy Tyner *(bottom right)* and drummer Elvin Jones. Some years ago he mastered the infrequently used soprano saxophone *(above, left)*.

These embattled mid-'60s avant-gardists briefly banded together as the Jazz Composers Guild *(left to right):* Jon Winter, Burton Greene, Bill Dixon, Le Sun Ra, Paul Bley, Roswell Rudd, Carla Bley, Mike Mantler, Cecil Taylor, John Tchicai, Archie Shepp—a good sampling of those who'd like a chance to work and be heard.

In 1964-5, Coltrane encouraged recordings by several of the most forward-minded. These "new thing" dates were mostly built around tenor sax Archie Shepp, shown *(far left)* in consultation with 'Trane; with tenor Albert Ayler *(above);* with Roswell Rudd and John Tchicai *(above right).* Also on hand *(right):* trumpeters Charles Tolliver and young veteran Freddy Hubbard.

Among the new wave of pianists: Paul Bley

"There can be no neat summing-up at this point, for which one should be thankful. If there could be, it would have to mean that jazz was complete; or, in other words, dead. But that is far from the case. . . ."

Those words opened the final paragraph of the first (1955) edition of this book. We went on to note that Chet Baker was the choice as the subject of the final picture, although the bet was hedged by the comment: "within a year, this closing spot might better belong to someone else."

The quickly shifting tides and emphases of jazz may very well make any new choice every bit as vulnerable as that one proved to be. However, the present selection seems not only suitable, but safe. Ornette Coleman has already spearheaded a jazz revolution. Even if time should prove his revolution less consequential than it might seem now, or his role in it less vital, Coleman can still qualify as an effective symbol of the truth that jazz is, above all, change and movement. Hopefully, jazz can move forward without losing contact with its own past—and possibly a book such as this one can help in that respect. But with or without remembrance of the past, inevitably jazz has changed, does change, will change again.

Thus it is more than reasonably certain that this is just the last page for the time being (which was the case last time); it is not The End.

INDEX

PICTURE SOURCES

The direct sources of the pictures in this book are listed here, page by page. Where several pictures appear on one page, the sequence of credits is always left-to-right, top-to-bottom. To avoid undue repetition, all sources listed more than once have been coded by initials; full identification of those through whose courtesy this material is used, in alphabetical order, is as follows:

ABC—ABC-Paramount Records
AR—Atlantic Records
GA—George Avakian
KB—Katherine Basie (Mrs. Count Basie)
BN—Blue Note Records
JB—Jack Bradley
CC—Charlie Campbell
CR—Columbia Records
TD—Thomas A. Dorsey
DB—Down Beat
LF—Leonard Feather
GH—George Hoefer
MGM—MGM/Verve Records
JRM—J. Robert Mantler photo
MM—Metronome Magazine
TM—Turk Murphy
RP—Robert Parent photo
TP—Tony Parenti
RCA—RCA-Victor Records
FR—Frederic Ramsey, Jr. (from the book *Jazzmen*)
RC—The Record Changer
RR—Riverside Records
HRC—The Herman Rosenberg Collection
SS—Steve Schapiro photo
DSc—Duncan Scheidt
DoSc—Don Schlitten photo
CS—Cecil Scott
NS—Nat Shapiro
CSt—Charles Stewart photo
ES—Dr. Edmond Souchon
DSt—David Stuart
GWa—George Wallington
PW—Pete Welding
GW—George Wettling

Chapter 1: 2—ES. 4 and 5—all RC. 6—FR; DSt. 7—FR; RC. 8 and 9—all ES. 10—ES; GH. 11—two GH; FR. 12—GH; two DSt. 13 and 14—all GH. 15—GH; FR; ES. 16—two GH; ES. 17—RC; DSt.

Chapter 2: 18—GH. 20 and 21—all ES. 22—GH; ES. 23—RC; GH; RC. 24—top RC; others TP. 25—both ES. 26—ES; RR. 27—GH; RC.

Chapter 3: 28—DSt. 30—GH; RC. 31—RR; RC. 32—DSt. 33—FR; two RC. 34—Sidney Desvignes; Lawrence Duhe. 35—Robert Koester. 36—both GH. 37—RC; two GH. 38 through 41—all GH. 42—three GH; three RC. 43—top RR; others GH. 44 and 45—all GH.

Chapter 4: 46—MM. 48—all RC. 49—A.P. Bedou; GH. 50—Muggsy Spanier, from FR. 51—GA; FR. 52—GH; RC; MM. 53 to 55—all RC. 56—RC; MM; CR. 57—Carole Reiff Galletty photo.

Chapter 5: 58—RC. 60—Roy J. Carew; two RC. 61—GH. 62—RCA; RC. 63—DSt. 64—DSt; RC. 65—DSt. 66—three RC; CC. 67—RC.

Chapter 6: 68—GH/DB. 70—GH; TD. 71—GH. 72—RC; TD. 73—four RCA; Ray Flerlage photo, from Delmark Records; Piedmont Records. 74—FR. 75—DSc; RCA; PW; RC. 76—all PW. 77—PW; RC; two MGM. 78—PW; Flerlage photo, from PW; RC; CR; MM. 79—MM; ABC.

Chapter 7: 80—RCA. 82—GH; RCA; RC; JRM; RC. 83—HRC; William Russell; MM. 84—HRC; RC. 85—RCA.

Chapter 8: 86 and 88—GH. 89—RR; two RC; GH; GW. 90—MM; two GW. 91—two GH; RC. 92—three RC; GH. 93—JRM; RC.

Chapter 9: 94—GH. 96—GH; RR. 97—two RR; GH. 98—MM; two RC; DB. 99—DB. 100—RC; RCA. 101—GH; RC.

Chapter 10: 102 and 104—RC. 105—RC; GH. 106—GH. 107—two GH; DSc. 108—two HRC. 109—HRC; two RC. 110—HRC; CS. 111—RC; HRC. 112—both Hal Flakser. 113—both GH. 114—GH; RC. 115—RC; DSc.

Chapter 11: 116—MM. 118—MM; GH; HRC. 119—HRC; RC. 120—RC; RR. 121—MM; RC; two HRC. 122—all RC. 123—MM. 124—two MM; GA. 125—GH.

Chapter 12: 126—RC. 128—RC; DB; MM. 129—CS; HRC. 130—RC. 131—HRC; RC. 132—two RCA; Ed Kirkeby; RCA; DSc. 133—RCA; GH. 134—RCA, RC; GH; two RC. 135—RC.

Chapter 13: 136—RC. 138—RR; two RC. 139—RC. 140—Charles Sutherland; MM; two RCA; 141—MM; GH; HRC. 142—three RC; two RCA; MM. 143—GH; MM; two RC. 144—MM; GH; RCA. 145—RCA; MM; RC. 146—RCA; JB. 147—MGM.

Chapter 14: 148 and 150—both KB. 151—two RC; GH. 152—MM; GH; RC. 153—both KB.

Chapter 15: 154—RCA. 156—both DB. 157—DB; RC. 158—GH; RCA. 159—RC; MM. 160—RCA; GH. 161—GH; MM. 162—MM; GH; MM. 163—two MM; GH. 164—MM; RCA. 165—two MM; RCA; MM. 166—MM; RC. 167—MM. 168—GH; MM. 169—all MM. 170—both GH. 171—NS; GH. 172—two RC; RCA. 173—RC; NS; LF. 174—NS; GH. 175—two MM; RC; RCA. 176—DB; RCA. 177—DB; MM; RC; GH. 178—both RCA. 179—RC; DB; HRC. 180—both MM. 181—LF; MM; RCA. 182—MM; RCA. 183—RC; GA.

184—MM; GH. 185—GH; HRC. 186—HRC; DB; MM. 187—JRM; MM; GH; LF. 188—MM; CR; RC. 189—both MM. 190—JB; RC. 191—RCA.

Chapter 16: 192 and 194—all RC. 195—GH; MM. 196—RC. HRC. 197—RC; JRM. 198—DSc; JRM. 199—JRM. 200—MM; HRC. 201—all RC. 202—LF; DSc. 203—both RC. 204—RC; RCA; JRM; RC. 205—MM; RC; Joe Sullivan; JRM. 206—JRM. TP/JB. 207—both JB.

Chapter 17: 208—GH. 210—both RC. 211—RC; two GH. 212—RC; GH. 213—RC. 214—all JRM. 215—TM; ES. 216—RC; MGM. 217—GA; MGM. 218—MGM; two RC. 219—AR; two RC. 220—two ES; RC; JB. 221—ES; two RC; two JB.

Chapter 18: 222—RC. 224—RC; TM; RC. 225—two RC; TM. 226—RC; Good Time Jazz Records. 227—RC; CC; GH; two RC. 228 and 229—all RC.

Chapter 19: 230—RC. 232—MM; LF. 233—both LF. 234—GWa; LF. 235—two MGM; GWa. 236—all MGM. 237—MGM; MM; MGM. 238—CR; MM. 239—RC. 240—RC; DSc; RC. 241—MM; two CSt; MM. 242—RC; MM; RC; MGM. 243—GH; two RC. 244—Jean Failows/JB; two RC. 245—LF; MGM. 246—RC; MM; DB. 247—MM; MGM; RCA; RC. 248—RC; RCA; MM. 249—DB; MM. 250—GH; RCA; two RC; MM. 251—DB; CR; DB. 252—DB; MM; DoSc. 253—RCA; CSt; MM. 254—NS; RC. 255—RC.

Chapter 20: 256—CR. 258—all CR. 259—JB; William Claxton photo, from DB; MGM; Claxton photo, from MM. 260—Claxton photo, from LF; CSt; MM. 261—CR; two MGM; RC. 262—AR; RC; MM; RC. 263—DoSc; RR; CR. 264—two AR; MGM. 265—MGM; SS; LF. 266—MM; LF. 267—MM; SS; CR; SS; CR. 268—SS; CR; two SS. 269—all SS. 270—RP; CR; JB. 271—CR; three MGM. 272—CR; AR; MGM; AR. 273—two MM; RP. 274—MM; CSt; CR; SS. 275—CSt; SS; MM; three SS. 276—three MM; SS. 277—JB; MM; CSt; DoSc. 278—MM; ABC; MM. 279—MGM; two CSt. 280—MM; MGM; CSt; SS. 281—CSt; SS; CR; RR; AR; SS. 282—two SS; CSt; CR; two DB; MGM. 283—two SS; DB; MGM. 284—SS; DB; MGM; DB; CSt. 285—SS; CSt; MGM; CSt. 286—CR; MGM; four SS. 287—CSt; SS; MM; two SS; CSt. 288—DB; two AR; JB. 289—all DB. 290—DoSc; SS; CR; DoSc; CR. 291—CSt; ABC; CSt. 292—DB; four CSt; DB. 293—AR.